THE UNHAPPY HERO

A Revealing Insight into the Turbulent Life of Lars Elstrup, Danish Darling and Luton Town Striker

Carsten Fog Hansen
and Jens Rasmussen

pitch

First published by Pitch Publishing, 2024

Pitch Publishing
9 Donnington Park,
85 Birdham Road,
Chichester,
West Sussex,
PO20 7AJ
www.pitchpublishing.co.uk
info@pitchpublishing.co.uk

A CIP catalogue record is available for this book from the British Library.

ISBN 978 1 80150 662 5

Typesetting and origination by Pitch Publishing

Printed and bound in India by Replika Press Pvt. Ltd.

Contents

Preface 11

1. Goodbye Football. 17
2. The Soft Boy From Råby. 25
3. Anxiety-Filled Success in the Big City 41
4. A Brief Visit to Brøndby 53
5. Hell in the Netherlands. 71
6. Falling in Love With Odense, and Finding Joy With the National Team 88
7. From Odense to Luton 100
8. The Reborn Goalscorer. 116
9. Heading to the Euros. 138
10. The Unhappy Hero 151
11. Anxiety 167
12. Sangha and the New Life. 175
13. From Elstrup to Darando. 186
14. The Converted 191
15. A Black Hole 199
16. The Depression Disappears. 206
17. Blue Rope and Roller Skates 217
18. New Downfall, New Beginning, New Depression, New Start. 226
19. The Sanctuary of 2012 243

Epilogue: 11 years on – Revival of Luton and Lars . . 248

Facts and Statistics 254

Bibliography 255

Dedication

Carsten Fog Hansen

First and foremost, a big thank you goes to Lars Elstrup for being willing to participate in this project. For generously and honestly sharing of himself and his life story. It has been a pleasure to get to know such a complex and interesting person.

Furthermore, a special thanks goes to family, friends and former team-mates who, in various ways, have contributed to this book and, each in their own way, have helped to add nuance to the picture of Lars.

A big thank you to Informations Forlag, our Danish publisher, who believed in the project and provided support and encouragement to a debutant author. In this regard, a special thanks to Jens 'Jam' for embracing the project and using his experienced pen to help elevate the story to the level it deserves. Also a big thank you to Pitch Publishing, for believing in and supporting this updated English version of the book

Last but not least, a special thank you to my wife, Louise. It has required time and patience to be married to a man who, in addition to his regular full-time job, has spent many evenings, days, and weekends researching and writing this book. But I have never lacked support or encouragement on the home front and therefore feel like a deeply privileged husband.

Dedication

Jens 'Jam' Rasmussen

A heartfelt thank you to:

Lars Elstrup, for participating, for open and interesting conversations, and for giving enjoyable company.

Carsten Hansen, Mette Jokumsen, and Informations Forlag for their extensive groundwork and trust in my writing abilities. And for the good collaboration, of course.

My three Norwegian girls, who once again witnessed me immersing myself in the writing process: Mathilde Jensine, Frida Sofie, and Kari Anne.

The Norwegian InnerLife therapists Anne Kristin Sjøli and Linda Falch, who have provided me with inspiration and insights into psychotherapy.

Teachers, residents, and guests at the Buddhist Center Copenhagen, for their transmissions, teachings, kindness, and inspiration.

Various kind people who, on the path to the deadline, have encouraged and expressed their interest in this book.

My mother, Karen Møller Rasmussen, who has occasionally offered office space and an internet connection.

Preface

OF COURSE, we all know Lars Elstrup. Every football enthusiast in Denmark over the age of 30 does. We still remember how time almost stood still on that June evening in 1992 when Elstrup irresistibly moved forward at the near post and put Flemming Povlsen's cross into the French goal, sending Denmark to the European Championship semi-finals.

This goal, this victory, the drama of the semi-final where Elstrup scored a penalty, and the subsequent triumph in the European Championship are collective memories of historical happiness in Denmark. The European Championship Final victory stands as the greatest unifying event since Denmark's liberation from German occupation on the evening of 4 May 1945.

Or almost unifying. Because for at least one Dane, the final was an overwhelming experience of anxiety and isolation.

The story of Lars Elstrup is not just the story of one of the country's best football players. It is the story of a suffering human being's search for his inner values despite the demands of the outside world and his increasingly troublesome depressions. Afflictions that not only challenge Elstrup's mood but also his life.

Just as clearly as Elstrup's pivotal goal sits in our memory, so does his subsequent downfall that shook Danish football in the years after the European Championship triumph. First, when he abruptly ended his football career just over a year after the final, at the age of only 30. Then, when he withdrew from society and joined the religious sect, Sangha (Solens Hjerte), changing his name to Darando.

It was no less shocking when he attempted a comeback in top-level football as a 37-year-old after a seven-year hiatus at the beginning of the new millennium. And again, when he excelled with a few controversial 'happenings' that put him back in the media headlines.

At that time, the authors of this book, like most others, thought that the former star was truly losing his grip. And no less so when he appeared in the media throughout the 2000s with stories of setbacks, suicide attempts, and internal and external conflicts.

But all along, each of us has had a thinly veiled curiosity to get to know Lars Elstrup better, to go beyond the newspaper headlines and the happenings he has performed, to find out who he is.

Why has he made the choices in life that he has? What have these choices done to him? What troubles him, and what makes him happy?

That has been the motivation: to tell a deeper story about Lars Elstrup. The life story of a man whose battle with his dark side has been harsher and more demanding than any important and gruelling football match.

All this without forsaking the biography of one of the country's best strikers in the late 1980s and early '90s. Because football, the game with the ball and the dynamics between team-mates and opponents, is a lifelong love for both us as authors and certainly for Lars as well.

At the same time, Lars's story is more relevant than ever. We first wrote this book in Danish, back in 2012, only three years after the German national team goalkeeper Robert Enke committed suicide after struggling with depression for six years. We had been in the process of writing it when the Welsh national team coach and former top player Gary Speed also took his own life. Around the same time, former Hull City player Dean Windass revealed that he had attempted suicide after battling depression for the past couple of years.

After the book came out, there were more stories in the same mould. Clarke Carlisle, the former Burnley and Watford defender, notably addressed his mental health struggles and attempts on his own life around 2014, while former striker Marvin Sordell revealed his battles with depression in 2017.

In April 2017, Aaron Lennon, the English winger who has played for clubs including Tottenham Hotspur and Everton, was detained by police under the UK's Mental Health Act due to concerns about his wellbeing. He was found on the side of a road in a distressed state and was subsequently taken to a hospital for assessment. In 2018 Danny Rose – the English left-back, capped 29 times by his country – spoke candidly about his battle with depression, which was triggered by a combination of injury and family tragedy and in the same vein.

Depression and suicide, it seems, is also a part of top-level sport, just like in general life and society. And although not all mental battles end up costing those involved their lives, it often ends up costing them their careers. To this last category, we can add names like German national team player Sebastian Deisler and Elstrup himself. Perhaps also Paul Gascoigne as well.

Depression and suicide attempts are often associated with taboo, both among the general population and especially among elite athletes. As expectations and salaries for players rise, and idolisation reaches new heights, it may also become harder for us spectators to accept that the players – although financially rich and famed – are ordinary people with weaknesses like the rest of us. And one may wonder if it is the players themselves who should be able to 'show weakness' and ask for help. Can they do that at all in a macho-fixated world? In a results-oriented performance culture where it is more important for us as spectators that they perform on the field than reveal their vulnerability to a psychologist or therapist?

For us authors, this book is a humble contribution to the debate on how we actually treat our heroes. Since Robert Enke's suicide, Germany has taken the initiative to start the Robert Enke Foundation, an organisation that seeks to help players with mental problems. Many clubs abroad have employed psychologists and even priests, knowing that the players' wellbeing is not just about the state of their gear and their physical condition, but about their entire being, their inner wellbeing. It would be commendable and joyful if we can move in the same direction here at home.

We hope that this story will present a more nuanced picture of the human being and football player that is Lars Elstrup. Neither better, worse, more, nor less normal or abnormal than he is.

Fortunately, Lars agreed to participate in this project. The first version of this book was based on a series of interviews conducted in 2011 and 2012, in which Lars openly and honestly spoke with the authors about his ups and downs. We supplemented it with conversations with his parents and some of his former team-mates. Without Lars's time and the participation of these generous individuals, the book wouldn't have been made.

After the first version of this book came out in Denmark in June 2012, its significance and the impression it left on those who read it made us increasingly consider over time whether it should reach a broader audience. Even if people couldn't necessarily identify with the choices Lars had made, the mental battles and the yearning for inner peace resonated. Likewise, in Denmark, the book made a notable contribution to the debate about the importance of seeing footballers as whole individuals.

Beyond this, there has also been a longing among us for this story to be read by fans of the club that held such great significance for Lars himself. He stayed at Luton Town for just two years, but he left a lasting impression on the club's fans with his 19 league goals in 60 games, and a massive contribution in saving Luton from relegation in the 1990/91 season.

But it wasn't only Lars who left a lasting mark on Luton. Luton also left a lasting mark on Lars.

While his depressions and struggles didn't cease during his time at Luton, he vastly enjoyed the time with team-mates, and fans of Luton, who he found engaging and passionate, yet never ever unpleasant. Also, the more relaxed approach to life as a professional footballer he encountered there was in stark contrast to what he faced during his first overseas stint at Feyenoord. So even though the battles off the pitch continued for Lars, there was no doubt that his strong performances on the field for Luton were a direct result of experiencing a freedom and joy in the game there.

It is therefore a great pleasure for us that this updated version of the book, including a new final chapter, is now available to fans of Luton Town as well as a wider audience of English-speaking readers.

Carsten Fog Hansen and Jens 'Jam' Rasmussen
August 2023

1
Goodbye Football

'EVER SINCE I signed my first contract, I've been considering how I could get out of it.'

It's a mild summer day in 1993, and the man behind these words is leaving his large apartment at the intersection of Kongensgade and Dronningensgade in downtown Odense. Determined, he walks towards Odense Boldklub's office, located further up Kongensgade, just a few minutes' walk from his apartment. Not much time to change his mind. But that doesn't matter. The man has made his decision. And it's final. Now he just needs to announce it to the public. One fax to the country's leading sports editorial offices, and it will be done. Over.

In the fax, the man will announce his immediate and sensational retirement as a professional football player. Sensational because it involves a mere 30-year-old national team player, European champion, Superliga star, former foreign professional, and star striker for the newly crowned Danish silver medal and cup winners.

He has formulated the wording of the fax in less than 20 minutes, but the considerations behind it have been brewing for years. Several years, in fact. In reality, he decided on retirement two years earlier. A lucrative contract in English top-level football was within reach, but instead, he chose to return to his hometown club, OB. A club he knew. In an environment where he felt at home. A fitting place to end his career. The two-year contract with OB would be his last in his professional career. He knows it. He has made his decision. In the summer of 1993, it's over.

No more professional football for Lars Elstrup.

Preparation

In the summer of 1991, Lars returned to Denmark after two seasons with the then English First Division club Luton Town. And now, at least mentally, he can sense that he is nearing the end as a professional football player. Sporting-wise, the past year in the small town 30 miles north-west of London has been sufficiently successful, and he has scored plenty of goals. But over the two seasons in the top professional game, the daily competition has taken its toll on Lars's worn psyche. Increased performance anxiety has planted poisonous doubts in his fragile mind. Doubts that nag at him and increasingly challenge his fundamental joy of the game. And it's not just his goalscoring ability and experience from English football that he brings back across the North Sea to the pride of Funen, Odense Boldklub. Deep melancholy also permeates his otherwise celebrated existence at the club. But only Lars himself knows what stirs beneath the surface. Inside him. And it's not anything particularly positive. He feels mentally trapped. Lacking joy. In football. In daily life. In life itself.

Everyone knows Lars Elstrup. At least, they know the football player Elstrup. His retirement will undoubtedly attract attention and ignite speculation in the sports press. The retirement will seem sudden, surprising, and peculiar to all football enthusiasts in the country. Just a few months after his 30th birthday and a week and a half after the season ended as a star for the Danish league runners-up. A little over a year after his goal sent Denmark to the European Championship semi-finals. And where his intuition and successful penalty kick contributed to Denmark's sensational appearance in the final.

But Lars is preparing for his farewell. He feels it inside. That's what he wants. What he desires. Because behind the predominantly successful facade, Lars has been struggling with his many anxiety attacks and severe depressions, even in the midst of the most celebrated match in Danish football history.

However, it is not that experience or other mentally burdensome incidents that he wants to justify his retirement with. And he doesn't need to because he can give another, less suspicious reason for his retirement: his chronic knee problems. Nothing mysterious about it. He is far from the first top player who has had to retire before the expected date due to physical injuries. And after 12 senior seasons with gruelling physical demands, bone-threatening tackles, and ligament-testing obstacles, Lars knows that. And the people around him can understand it too. Or so he hopes. But for Lars, the knee problems are just the excuse he has been waiting for, for years.

The smile that disappeared

The truth is, for about as many years as a football player usually dreams of victories and success, he has mostly wished to be free from it all. Wished to be freed from the burdensome yoke that being a professional has often been for him.

But he has still held on to his professional career. Hoping to get better over time. With himself, the professional football environment, performance anxiety. But he has also held on to the career to not disappoint or let anyone down. Team-mates, club management, his father, the fans, friends, and himself.

But now he can't take it any more. His body and mind are worn out.

In particular, the latter has left its mark on him. Over a longer period, he has been feeling worse and worse. His warm smile has long receded into the background. Erased by anxiety, worry, and melancholy.

'At that time, I was 30 years old and couldn't smile. When I walked down the street and saw other people smiling. I thought, "I would also like to smile again!"' reflects Lars.

It's not like people have noticed the absence of his smile. Lars has played his role as the cheerful football player to the fullest. He has put on the right face, complied, and done what was expected of him. And he has played the role so well that he has even fooled those closest to him.

'When people see pictures of me from back then, they say, "But you were such a happy guy and always so nice to be around. You were smiling and at the top of your career!" But my smile wasn't genuine,' he says. Lars also didn't let his then partner Charlotte get close enough to share in his inner thoughts and concerns.

'I am just like that or I grew up thinking that you can't talk to others about anything or any problems. So everything was kept inside me. I couldn't express myself, and I felt that when I said something, it was completely wrong,' Lars continues, beginning his reasoning about the lack of dialogue about his problems, in relationships and life in general.

'I remember one time when Charlotte wanted to talk to me at the dining table. She could sense that something was wrong with me, but all I could think about was when I could get away from that table and out the door because I didn't want to talk to anyone about anything.

'And it would have been a defeat in advance if, for example, I had sought out a psychologist. It would have shown signs of weakness if I had needed help, right? That was completely out of the question for me to talk to a psychologist or, for that matter, any other person because then others could use it against me. So even that was completely out of the question in the world I lived in.'

Not even among his team-mates at Odense has anyone noticed anything. The contrast between Lars's status in the side as a national team player and top scorer and his own self-perception is enormous.

'I was the star of the team, but I was afraid to go to training, afraid to play a match, afraid to drive a car, afraid to be out in society. I trembled at the thought of having to perform,' he recalls.

But now it has to end. Lars has made his decision. The season is over, and his contract with OB has expired. He has been plagued by injuries in the past season and feels justified in quitting football. But deep down, he also has no desire to stand up and formally bid farewell. He just wants to get away from it all. To disappear, and find himself and his own space. He doesn't want to have to answer a lot of questions.

On the other hand, he feels that he owes the world an explanation. After all, he is a popular figure among OB's fans. Not least for his friendly nature but also because he has made a significant contribution to the team with 24 goals in 44 matches, helping them secure the national cup and a place in Europe.

The broader public also vividly remembers how Elstrup secured Denmark a place in the European Championship semi-finals in June 1992 with his winning goal against France. That goal has for ever cemented his name in Danish football history and made him popular among the football-loving Danes, who have also enjoyed 12 other Elstrup goals in the national team jersey. He is aware of all this. The expectations of the world are not new to him. That's why he chooses to announce his retirement via fax instead of simply disappearing.

'I was a public figure and a well-known name. That's why I felt that I had to announce my retirement instead of just disappearing without resurfacing,' says Lars.

The decision has been made and cannot be changed. Lars just needs to send the fax. And although he has had the decision in his thoughts for a long time, he hasn't shared it with anyone except Charlotte.

'Because it was a decision I was happy to have made and could stand by. And you like to share good things with your girlfriend,' Lars admits.

Space ahead

In essence, he has kept the decision a secret because he didn't want people to try to talk him out of it. At OB, he is still a valuable asset. Perhaps one of the best players the club has ever had. He will be very difficult to replace, and director Jørgen Bækkelund has been pressuring Elstrup for a contract extension. After all, he is only 30 years old and has several good seasons left in him as a player, Bækkelund reminds him. Despite the increasing injuries, Elstrup's main strength, his goalscoring ability, remains intact, and he has been among the Superliga's top performers in the past season. There would even be room for Elstrup to lower his level a bit or play fewer minutes and still make a significant contribution to OB's first team. But he has rejected any extension.

He puts the concise A4 page in the fax machine and presses the send button. The paper with the announcement slowly makes its way through the machine and spreads out to the country's sports editorial offices. Now it's done. Now the message is out there, and they can all think what they want. The press, team-mates, the club, family, fans. He lets out a sigh of relief, takes a moment to gather his thoughts, and prepares to leave the office at OB, his last football club. He wants to get away quickly. He has already planned a summer vacation with his girlfriend and has no desire to be confronted about his decision. He doesn't want to deal with the reactions that will inevitably come once his decision is known. Perhaps the journalists will inquire about the content of the fax? Maybe even dig into whether the chronic injuries are the sole reason for his retirement? He's not ready for that. And he doesn't want to answer any more questions.

As he is leaving, the office phone rings. It's the first journalist calling. The experienced Torben Larsen from daily newspaper *BT*, whom Lars has a good relationship with. Larsen wants to meet Elstrup for an interview but is turned down. He can read what's in the press release. But yes, the decision is final, and nothing can change it, Lars asserts in his brief comment.

Lars still doesn't know what he will do next. He has been playing football since he was six years old. For the past seven years, he has made a living from it. He could return to working in a bank, but changing jobs is not something he is considering at all. He doesn't need it either. His football career has earned him enough money, and he doesn't have to work for many years. But those thoughts haven't dominated him or motivated his decision.

'At that time, I had no plans for the future, and I wasn't thinking about spiritual seeking either,' says Lars.

'What I thought about was that something was wrong, and now it had to be enough. I needed to distance myself from something that wasn't good for me, something that prevented me from smiling.

'Along the way in the decision-making process, I also thought about Lasse Skov, my former team-mate, who had taken a sabbatical period where he sailed around in his own boat in the Mediterranean. It had triggered a lot of thoughts in me because that was precisely the kind of space I was looking for. A place where you could breathe a little easier, regain your composure, or feel better in some way.

'But the most important thing was the feeling of finding a sanctuary. The feeling of being free, not bound by anything or any contract. Not having to do anything. Not having to go to training or show up at work. But being able to be myself and do the things I truly wanted to do.'

Initially, the space is set in his in-laws' summer house in Hasmark on the island of Funen. Lars spends a long and pleasant summer vacation there with Charlotte, filled with romance, beach trips, and enjoying ice-cream. Plenty of free time, the numbing feeling of freedom, no football matches. Space for Lars Elstrup.

2

The Soft Boy From Råby

WHEN YOU take the beautiful drive from Randers northwards along Udbyhøjvej, you eventually end up at the mouth of Randers Fjord. Just before this estuary, you pass through the small village of Råby, home to barely 300 people and many more chickens and cows.

Despite its remoteness and small size, the village boasts the country's largest village pond. At 15,000 square metres, the pond forms an impressive centrepiece. But it also has a practical history. Originally, the locals extracted clay from the pond to build the first houses in the area. Later, the pond was used when the farmers' horse-drawn wagons, barrels, and other agricultural tools became too dry or loose at the joints. Wagons, barrels, and tools were simply thrown into the pond so that the wood could become wet and expand again.

Later, the school was built next to the pond. It then became a preferred playground for the school's children, who enjoyed jumping over stacks of clay stones drying on a small 'half-island' in the middle of the pond.

The pond, the rural atmosphere, and Råby's scenic location between fields and fjord easily evoke thoughts of idyllic old movies. And one senses that things move at a more patient pace here than in the neighbouring city of Randers, about a 20-minute drive to the west.

But Råby is not only known for the pond. It is also here that the man who would later secure a semi-final spot for the Danish national football team at the 1992 European Championship grew up. It is here that Lars Elstrup is shaped, for better or worse. It is from here that his journey begins.

Today, like many other towns in the Danish outskirts, Råby has fallen victim to the retail decline, which has hit smaller towns particularly hard. The small shops that constituted its commercial street have closed one after another, and only a few stores remain.

One of the surviving shops is the grocery store, located centrally. Upon entering, one quickly senses that it is not only people from Råby who shop there. It is busy, and the store is full of life. While the surrounding grocery shops have closed down over the years, this one stands as a steadfast and lonely survivor. For several decades, it was personified by Tage Elstrup, the store manager for over 35 years until the diligent man's retirement in the mid-1990s.

The grocery store and the brothers

Tage Elstrup arrived in Råby on a cold November day in 1961 at the age of 24. He himself was born and raised in nearby Udbyhøj as the son of the local forester. Tage had no great desire to move away, and it suited him well to take over the local grocery store not far from his childhood home. To Råby he took his wife Ingelise, seven years younger than him, and their newborn son, Peter. Ingelise was born in Copenhagen and spent her first three months in the capital but grew up in Brenderup near Middelfart and later attended a domestic science school. They met in 1959 at the Cooperative School in Middelfart, where Tage was a student and Ingelise worked as a kitchen maid, helping with cooking and serving meals to the school's approximately 90 students. Ingelise got to know Tage from their daily interactions, but it was not until a later ball that they ended up becoming a couple.

Like so many other families in the early 1960s, the newlyweds lived in a fairly traditional manner. Ingelise was the diligent wife, taking care of the home and their son, while Tage worked to provide for their daily needs.

The family quickly settled into the small town, and Tage successfully ran the local grocery store, earning the respect and customer loyalty of the locals. In the coming years and decades, the Elstrup family would leave their mark on Råby. They displayed their entrepreneurial spirit, business acumen, community involvement, and a special knack for the game of football.

Shortly after the family's arrival in Råby, Ingelise had even more to attend to on the home front. On Sunday, 24 March 1963, around noon, Lars Dahl Elstrup came into the world through a home birth. And it was with great pride that the parents welcomed their second son, just 18 months after the arrival of the first.

The small age difference between Peter and Lars would allow the two brothers to enjoy each other's company throughout their childhood and youth. In and around the small countryside town, there were plenty of opportunities for movement, imaginative play, and all sorts of ball games, primarily their greatest passion: football. The Elstrup family's garage also made room for table tennis, billiards, and foosball, and board games and playing cards were enjoyed in the boys' room.

Lars admired Peter and looked up to him. The phrase 'just like Peter' was a regular part of his everyday life, whether it involved choosing clothes or other ordinary activities. However, the two boys also had their differences, clear and distinct. While Peter would spring out of bed in the morning, Ingelise often had to wake Lars more than once to get him up and off to school. The differences between the outgoing Peter and the introverted Lars became more evident as they grew up as boys, teenagers, and young men.

When Peter, at the age of seven or eight, was about to start taking dance lessons, Ingelise asked Lars if he wanted to join. But he adamantly refused. 'I was just determined not to do it. I thought I would look so silly, foolish, and awkward on a dance floor and become a total laughing stock in front of the girls and everyone else,' he recalls, not failing to add a light self-ironic laugh.

But that's just how Lars, the boy, was – shy and introverted.

Music and field burning

Music, in general, wasn't Lars's thing, and he only acquired one record from the diverse palette of popular music genres in the 1970s, such as beat, glam rock, heavy metal, disco, punk, and pop.

'The only LP record I ever bought was one by ABBA. *Waterloo.* Is there a record with that title? But I bought that record because I thought if I wasn't interested in music, I would seem strange to those around me. So I bought this one record, and it was played once or twice,' Lars explains.

However, he doesn't fail to mention that as a boy, he was 'totally wild about and in love with the blonde from ABBA'.

But Peter listens to music, buys LPs, and twirls local girls around on the dancefloor. As an early teenager, he often arranges rendezvous with them in a bedroom or behind a bush in a warm and lush summer garden. Little Lars takes note when his older brother comes home from a party with dirty trousers and a satisfied smile on his face. Lars himself prefers to sit alone at home in his bedroom, with his favourite comic strip, *The Phantom*, or some of his collectibles: the popular NU pictures of Danish football players, temporary tattoos, or glossy pictures.

When Lars does make a little fuss, it's in less fortunate contexts. At the age of only 12, he has to be carried home from a New Year's Eve party at the local mission leader's son's house as early as 10pm. Instead of setting off his fireworks, he sleeps off his first hangover in his bed while 1975 turns into 1976.

On the other hand, Lars is privileged to have his fireworks delivered in the summer, a few years later. As the manager of the grocery store, Tage is the man who sells fireworks to the people of Råby. In midsummer, he is visited by a salesman who has product samples with him. Lars gladly receives a package of fireworks as a gift, although he has no intention of leaving it unopened until the end of the year.

That same summer, Lars eagerly shows his cousin Morten how to launch a rocket. The neighbouring field is filled with abundant, ripe, and dry crops. Like a guided missile, Lars's rocket flies straight into the neighbour's cornfield, which suddenly catches fire.

The adults are gathered around the lunch table when a desperate Lars rushes into the dining room, shouting, 'Dad, Dad, it's burning!' Tage replies, 'Burning? Can't you just throw a bucket of water on it?' Lars looks astonished at his father and replies, 'A bucket? No, Dad, that won't be enough!'

Father, mother, and the rest of the party quickly rise from the table. Outside the front door, they are met with a rather alarming sight: the neighbour's field is completely engulfed in flames. Lars's uncle, Steffen, tries to use a fire hose, but it's too late to save the field. The fire brigade is called in and prevents the blaze from spreading to the buildings. Meanwhile, the residents of Råby gather in large numbers around the burning field across from the Elstrup family's home. The reason for the commotion: the otherwise timid boy Lars and his early version of a new year's rocket.

Today, Tage laughs when he tells the story. And although Lars was naturally embarrassed and shaken at the time, he remembers that the drama had a rather amicable ending.

Lars admits, 'The same day the field burned down, my father and the neighbour farmer gathered in my father's office to discuss insurance matters. The farmer said, "The patch that burned has always yielded well." It was, of course, the best-quality grain he had standing right where it burned. He was well insured and didn't seem too upset. My father took it in his stride and with good humour. I, on the other hand, felt sorry for all the commotion I had caused by being careless and was certainly burdened with guilt.'

However, Lars is done shooting new year rockets in the summertime. Conversely, the episode doesn't become a launching pad for further 'commotion' in his life. In the following years, Lars remains a very quiet and shy boy who prefers not to draw attention to himself.

Traditional family patterns

The family's role distribution is quite traditional, with the dominant role being held by the father. Tage earns the money and has the final say in decisions. There's nothing unusual about that. Tage himself was brought up that way, as was his own father. Tage and Ingelise are perfectly fine with this division of roles, which is a common family structure in the surrounding society. The father's authority is unquestioned. However, when it is questioned, it is usually by Peter, who, more than Lars, displays elements of Tage's robust personality. Peter often has to face the consequences in the form of the physical punishment that many fathers of that time used to command respect. On the other hand, the more sensitive and introverted Lars never rebels against Tage's authority. He shares more of Ingelise's character, and a central part of that is deference to the family's absolute authority.

'My father was the dominant and decisive type, while my mother was the one who listened and did as she was told. Just like us boys. In many ways, it was a matter of keeping quiet, following orders, and doing as we were told, or else. That's how I experienced being a boy,' says Lars, who explains how Tage's authoritarian behaviour could manifest itself.

'If we were sitting in the living room for a family gathering, my father would just sit and watch his TV programmes. Sometimes we boys would say that we wanted to watch a specific programme§ on TV, but our request would go unheard. At some point, I got my own television, and instead, I would go to my room because I wanted to sit and watch what I felt like. But that wasn't respected by him, so my mother would come into my room to ask me to come back to the living room. First time, then second time, and then the third time, almost crawling and crying with a soft voice, "Lars, please come to the living room." Because she knew what would happen. Eventually, my father would come into my room, grab me by the nape of the neck, and pull me back to my place in the living room because it was time for us to have a good time as a family. That was his idea of what family togetherness should look like that evening.'

Today, Lars feels that Tage's authoritarian behaviour, in many ways, came to shape his self-image, especially during puberty and his early youth: 'Until I turned 25, I was afraid to talk to girls because I felt shy, awkward, foolish, and thought I sounded stupid. I didn't feel like I had anything to say, and it was impossible for me to believe that she could be interested in me. I had inferiority complexes, but at the same time, I felt that it wasn't OK to feel this insecurity and have these anxiety-filled thoughts. On the contrary, I was raised to be big and strong and not show any weakness or insecurity.'

However, Lars also has a more forgiving reflection on his father and his childhood, 'My father simply followed his conviction about how to raise his children based on what he had learned. And we never lacked anything in terms of food, clothing, transportation, or necessities in the family, so in that sense, my parents always provided what they could for their children.'

Additionally, the family had a lot of social interaction with Lars's paternal grandmother, who lived in nearby Udbyhøj and represented a sense of security for him.

'At Grandma's, there was always candy, cakes, fruit juice, and no critical words because she loved her grandchildren more than anything in the world. So, it was a kind of safe space, but it wasn't like I would talk to her or confide in her because I didn't do that with anyone. But she was close,' says Lars, whose paternal grandfather passed away when he was just a few months old, and whose maternal grandparents he mostly saw when they went on family vacations to Funen.

First match, early happening

While Tage fails to express his love verbally or in his presence with his sons, he demonstrates it through a deep involvement in their extracurricular activities, especially the most natural one, football. His dedication and enthusiasm often fills the

Elstrup family's house and garden with other children from the neighbourhood. They happily come by to participate in the many sports matches and activities that Tage organises. This socially unifying engagement is also evident when the family goes on holiday. For Tage, holiday doesn't mean relaxation in a hammock but rather a lot of activities that often benefit the children.

'If we went on a camping trip, which we did a lot, my father was a focal point,' recalls Lars. 'He organised a football match or a dart game, and he set up the framework for us children to participate, play, and have fun. Not just for my brother Peter and me, but also for other children. And we loved him for that. He, who always had a pump for the ball, who knew how to set up a goal, what rules we played by, and so on.'

It also happens more than once that children, often of different nationalities, stand in front of the Elstrup family's caravan early in the morning and shout, 'Tage, Tage, Tage!' Then the senior Elstrup gladly arranges football matches with 20 to 30 children on each team. Tage can do that, and Peter and Lars are proud of their father, who is naturally popular among the other children due to his engagement, both on holidays and at home in Råby.

The local sports community also benefits greatly from Tage's motivation. He is the driving force behind the merger of several local sports clubs, which leads to the formation of IF Fjorden. For many years, he leads the new association as chairman, later as treasurer, and for a long time as a coach for various youth teams. He is a serious and innovative coach who does his utmost to make training exciting and different, which makes him well-liked among the young players.

'The will to want gives the ability to achieve' is the motto he puts up in IF Fjorden's locker room. It is a slogan that characterises Tage's coaching style, his business acumen, and his way of being a father.

At the age of six, Lars also joins IF Fjorden, where Peter has already had his first time as an under-7s player. Initially, Lars primarily plays badminton, and he has a flair for a variety of sports. But in the end he chooses football since he and Peter already spend hours playing matches with the other children from the neighbourhood.

As the boys grow older, Peter appears to be the more talented of the two brothers. He is more technically skilled and runs more during matches compared to Lars, who often drifts away on the flank. However, it is not laziness that leads him to sit on the crossbar during one of his first matches for IF Fjorden. Nor is it a sudden and revolutionary need to show off. It is mostly something social.

'It's the first football match I can remember, where we played at Råby Stadium with tall grass and molehills on the field. We were around seven or eight years old, and I was on the same team as my brother Peter, who was an excellent dribbler, someone who could fool everyone, and Claus from my school class, who was the goalkeeper,' recalls Lars. 'When we immediately took a 2-0 or 3-0 lead, I didn't care any more because we would win anyway. And we did end up winning the match 21-0 or 22-0, where Peter scored 15 or 17 goals and surely assisted the rest.

'But I saw that Claus was a little lonely and didn't have anything to do in the goal. Instead, he started building small sandcastles inside the goal line, so I went down to him and sat on our own crossbar to keep him company. The opponent was never near our goal.'

The stunt immediately caught the attention of Tage, who went ballistic on the sidelines and ordered his son to get down.

This climb on to the crossbar may be seen as an early sign of Lars's later inclination to challenge the rules and initiate certain controversial happenings.

'An early happening? Perhaps, hehe. That's how it must have seemed to the parents who were watching,' comments Lars with a half-grinning face.

However, as he progresses through the youth leagues, he develops the more playful and skilled side of what turns out to be a significant football talent.

Football for better and worse

Although he may occasionally appear somewhat absent during matches, it doesn't mean that Lars is any less eager to win or surpass his older brother. The competitive environment that permeates the Elstrup household gradually influences young footballer Lars as well. Perhaps it is precisely the internal competition with Peter and a feeling that his older brother is not nearly as good as himself that inspires Lars to strive for improvement. When Peter accomplishes 100 ball juggles, Lars won't stop until he achieves 101.

'Back then, Peter scored more goals than Lars. But Lars was the serious one who learned to avoid mistakes, and that's why he went the furthest,' Tage reveals many years later in an interview with newspaper *BT*.

Peter Elstrup also confirms the intense competition between the two brothers. In May 2011, he tells *Randers Amtsavis*, a local newspaper, 'We were both competitive types who wanted to win at all costs, whether it was competing in foot tennis in the backyard, playing badminton, or cycling.'

Fresh in Ingelise's memory is the infamous spring day when she calls Lars in for dinner. He is in the midst of setting a new record for ball juggles when his mother's call causes him to drop the ball, resulting in a failed record attempt. A furious son subsequently enters the house to have his evening meal.

Competition thus permeates the household during the years when the boys are becoming young men. Neither Tage, Peter, nor Lars like to lose, and the fine old sports motto of 'win or lose with the same mindset' doesn't resonate much with the three testosterone-fuelled family members. Their attitude drives them to perform, win football matches, and pushes the village boys to develop into exceptionally skilled players.

But in the mind of the oldest and still dominant member of the pack, the reaction pattern after a defeat resonates in an unfortunate way many years later.

When Lars achieves success at the 1992 European Championship, Tage makes a statement that he would later come to regret. He tells *BT*, 'I was the team manager when the boys played for IF Fjorden. After a couple of junior matches where things didn't go well, I ordered the boys to run in front of the car back home to Råby, a three-kilometre run. I threatened them that they wouldn't get dinner if they didn't take the run. It certainly helped. They had to know I meant it.'

Today, Tage regrets his words, which were largely interpreted as if it was commonplace for the sons to run home in front of the car after a defeat.

'It was partly a joke. None of them ever ran the three kilometres home, and of course, they got dinner. But I have always demanded more from them and been more consistent than my wife,' Tage explains in an interview with *BT*, two years after the triumph at the European Championship.

Lars also remembers the infamous car and running trip from IF Fjorden's home field in Dalbyovre to Råby. However, it was only Peter who was allowed to run the three kilometres home, he recalls, while his little brother sat quietly in the slowly rolling car.

Today, in hindsight, Tage acknowledges that he would have acted differently toward his boys, and he has regretted the remark about the run home 'many times'.

While Peter quickly understands his father's signals, it is much more difficult for Lars. He struggles to thrive under his father's demanding mentality, something that Tage notices when describing Lars in connection with the 1992 European Championship, 'He is a good boy, calm and thoughtful, with his mother's calm temperament.'

But behind the calm exterior, Lars fights an internal battle with his father. He wants to speak up against him. He would like to confront the challenges that Peter confronts him with. And as his older brother dares to do.

Above all, Lars feels an internal urge to challenge the perpetual competition mentality that pervades their home. Just once in a while.

Peter continues to answer back to Tage and face the consequences. Lars doesn't. Not yet. The more reserved younger brother complies, but within him, the ingredients for the later confrontation against authority are forming. 'I had seen how my brother had to run home after the car if he didn't play properly. So my defence mechanism became shutting down and doing what was said,' Lars reveals in an interview with *Aktuelt* on 15 January 2001.

Today, Lars Elstrup navigates between the good and the bad when reasoning about the two-headed entity of 'competition mentality'.

He says, 'The competition mentality was a big part of our family. If you didn't win, my father could shout and scold. It's good to have a winning instinct, and competition mentality is not only negative. Wanting to win, to triumph, or to be the best is a good trait to have because it's better to experience victory than defeat. Furthermore, a competitive mentality can contribute to one's development and make one better and more skilled.

'But all of that is only good as long as it functions in a healthy way, where one can tolerate losing and still maintain a good mood instead of becoming angry, introverted, furious, or having other emotional outbursts. Or where one begins to taunt people or scold them because you can't win every time, and there will always be someone who is better than oneself on any given day. And a game is a play that should bring joy and experience regardless of the outcome.'

In the spotlight of Freja

However, the winning mentality in the Elstrup family also leads to both Lars and Peter becoming key players on IF Fjorden's top youth team. They score goals at will and lead the team to several significant victories. In their later teenage years, the prominent neighbouring league club, Randers Freja, begins to show interest in the brothers.

Lars recalls, 'Back then, I worked in my father's grocery store in the afternoons after school. One summer day, the youth leader, Junge Petersen, from Randers Freja showed up in the store. He was sitting and talking with my dad while I was restocking shelves. I was called into the office, and there Junge made it clear to my father and me that he wanted me to join Randers and play, preferably as soon as possible. My brother was also offered a transfer and he was ready for it, but I didn't feel like switching. I wanted to wait and see how Peter would do in the big club in the big city. Junge and my dad accepted that, and there was never any pressure from anyone for me to switch or when to do it.'

Lars didn't have much self-awareness of his own football skills. Nor did he have big naive dreams.

He adds, 'As a boy or young man, I never had an ambition to become a national team player or a professional football player. Sure, I thought I was good, but I never said it to anyone because I always thought I wasn't good enough. When other people like Junge Petersen looked at you, they could see that you were good or better than the others and could play at a higher level. But I never thought about it. I just enjoyed playing football.'

Lars continues at IF Fjorden in the familiar environment he knows while Peter takes the leap and switches to Randers Freja. However, Lars often goes into the city to watch Peter train. Junge Petersen and Freja still have their eye on the younger Elstrup, and after a match between IF Fjorden and Randers Freja, an enthusiastic Junge encourages Peter, 'Can't you get your brother to join us soon?!'

Lars has been toying during the match with Freja's right-back, who is described as a talented defender. Junge has spotted many young talents in his life, and he instinctively knows that the little kid dribbling around his skilful right-back has the potential to play at a higher level than IF Fjorden.

But Lars isn't easily persuaded. He is addicted to security and still enjoys being with his friends and playing football in Fjorden. And even though Peter seems to be thriving, the thought of switching to the area's biggest club in the big city is, in many ways, a daunting thought for Lars.

Lars recalls, 'Randers was the big city, and as a 16-year-old, I would never have thought of going there alone. It was unsafe to leave the small village with two to three hundred inhabitants and 600 pigs and go to Randers. We were farmers, and there, they studied, partied, went out, had girlfriends and boyfriends.'

Junge does his best to persuade Lars. He offers him, among other things, a spot on a coveted tour of England that Peter and the rest of the Randers team will go on shortly after Lars's standout match against Freja. But such offers still don't tempt Lars, who declines, stating that he 'doesn't want to take a spot away from another player'.

After six months of consideration and continued interest from Freja, Lars finally gathers the courage and chooses to switch to the blue-and-white-striped Freja jersey and a team playing in the junior division.

Lars says in justification of his decision after more than six months of initial scepticism, 'And why did I eventually switch to Randers Freja? Maybe because I thought that something had to happen and I wanted to test myself against bigger and better players. And when someone thought I was good enough for that level and showed interest in me, well, there must be something to it, right? You can't keep going to kindergarten for ever. You move up a grade to learn more.'

And there was much more than a new football world and 'moving up a grade' waiting for Lars in the capital of Jutland.

3

Anxiety-Filled Success in the Big City

IN RANDERS Freja, Lars is now about to play football at the highest youth level, with a prestigious club known for its highly successful youth work. As expected and to some extent feared, Randers Freja is a big transition from IF Fjorden. Therefore, Lars is a nervous young man when he attends his first training session at the club under the leadership of the legendary Junge Petersen.

'That's when I entered the world of "the big guys" in the city, where I was "the little one" from the countryside. I truly felt small, didn't feel like I could do anything, and thought the others were much better,' Lars recounts about the beginning of his Freja era.

Nevertheless, he remembers it as 'a good time', and of course, having his established brother Peter present was a significant advantage.

'With Peter, it became easier to fit into the new team and among the new team-mates. Things were already going well for him in the club, he was well-liked, received praise, and made friends. I could talk to him and ask him about things. And, of course, that was a huge help instead of being completely alone in the new club.'

Although he is nervous and feels small, Lars quickly shows that he is good enough. Once he and his new team-mates get into what it's all about – the game on the field – Lars stands up to the challenge and more. In addition to his innate talent, Lars has honed his skills in various ways: primarily through the countless training hours and tournament matches with IF Fjorden, but also from the numerous matches he played with innocent joy alongside Peter and the other boys from the neighbourhood in Råby. In addition, he has spoiled his technique and ball control through many playful and focused solo training sessions, where he stood for hours on his own, practising dribbles, ball control, and juggling. All of this means that he has no problems adapting to the new team and the higher level at Randers Freja. He quickly becomes a regular player, but not in the centre-forward position that he later successfully takes on in the Danish national team.

'I quickly joined the team, playing as a left-winger. When we had the ball, I would look over at our right-winger, Claus Bering, whom I looked up to. I tried to learn from him when to make runs, which positions to seek, and how to make myself available. I also had the advantage of being left-footed, which made it easy for me to cross the ball,' says Lars.

Lars's strength is neither speed nor fancy dribbles but rather something much simpler, 'My strength lies in keeping it simple. Having a good overview and playing the ball first-time to the right place. I never actually thought it was important for me to be the one scoring the goals.'

But goals quickly come for Lars. Despite playing on the wing, he often manages to be in the right place at the right time and get the final touch on the ball.

'Later on, I discovered that I had this goalscoring instinct,' Lars reveals. 'It probably stems from not overcomplicating things.

Others would dribble around until they lost the ball. I found it easier to just score the goal right away. Then we could get the ball back to the centre circle and start again!'

It sounds simple, and it looks simple when Lars scores goal after goal in the following years on the junior and youth teams at Randers Freja, and he continues to do so later, when he starts playing at the senior level at the age of 18.

Debut in the second division

As senior players, both Lars and Peter quickly join Randers Freja's first team, which competes in the second division. A few years before the Elstrup brothers' arrival, the club had won the national cup tournament and finished as runners-up in the Danish championship (both in 1973). However, the late 1970s prove to be challenging; in 1978, Freja are relegated from the first division and have to work their way back up from the third division to establish a strong first team. At the same time, the club is burdened with a million-dollar debt, and this period marks a turning point in Danish club football, as the traditional amateur values are challenged by the idea of professionalism.

In Lars's debut season with the first team, the traditional Jutland club is overshadowed by the emerging phenomenon of Brøndby IF. The suburban Copenhagen club, led by Freja's former youth team captain, Per Bjerregaard, has groundbreaking plans for professional football in Denmark. And the visionary Bjerregaard also has a plan for talented attacker Lars, as will later become apparent.

From 1981 to 1983, Lars and Peter are among the talented young players in Freja's first-team squad, under the guidance of the experienced and renowned Per Røntved. It is remarkable that the Elstrup brothers get to play alongside the then national team captain. After scoring 40 goals in 194 Bundesliga matches for Werder Bremen (as a sweeper!), the mighty Bayern Munich were interested in the Danish defensive icon. However, instead of continuing his career in the Bundesliga, the 31-year-old Røntved shocks the football world by choosing to play for Randers Freja in the Danish second division. For Røntved, the money and prestige of one of Europe's leading clubs matter far less than the pure joy he misses in football, as it is played and cherished in a good Danish club like Randers Freja.

Lars knows Røntved from their childhood days, collecting NU football cards where the young Røntved appears in Brønshøj's kit. Lars has also seen Røntved on TV multiple times, captaining the Danish national team. It is not surprising that Røntved becomes a player whom Lars greatly admires.

And not just for his football skills and vast experience on the field. Røntved possesses the admirable self-assurance that Lars himself yearns for. One particular episode stands crystal clear in Lars's memory: after an indoor game around Christmas, the Freja team gathers for the subsequent consumption of mulled wine and *æbleskiver* (Danish Christmas pastries). Røntved sits on the bench at one of the tables and asks a team-mate to toss an *æbleskive* over to him. The player promptly reacts and throws the pastry towards Røntved, who casually turns his hand under it, catches it securely, places it on his plate, dips it in jam and powdered sugar, and continues eating as if nothing happened.

'Imagine if he had dropped the *æbleskive*? He would have looked foolish. But my respect for him increased by 100 per cent,' recalls Lars, whose chronic insecurity still held him back from taking unnecessary chances and testing himself: at communal dinners or on the football field.

Like Lars, Røntved is a left-footed player, and a fascinated Elstrup notes how the captain kicks the ball with a stretched instep. During a league match, Lars sees Røntved take a corner kick with a stretched left instep. The ball doesn't curl outward from the opponents' goal as usual but goes hard and precisely into the most dangerous area right in front of the goal.

After the match, Lars asks Røntved how he manages to kick the ball in that manner. Røntved's answer is brief but encouraging, 'You can learn that too!'

'But I didn't really believe I could. At least, I didn't dare to try it when I was in Randers. I only learned the technique down in Holland a couple of years later,' says Lars.

During his period in the senior team at Randers Freja, Lars simply enjoys playing and having fun with the ball and has no intentions of making football his livelihood. At this point, it is nearly impossible, at least in Denmark, where although there is a shift in the otherwise rooted amateur culture, not even Per Bjerregaard has truly begun thinking in terms of full-time professionalism.

Old traditional clubs like Randers Freja still uphold values such as team spirit and volunteerism and remain sceptical of 'paid football', which many see as a threat to community life and healthy amateurism.

'I played as an amateur in Randers, and if we did well, we got a trip to Mallorca, which was a great incentive for us players. And even if we hadn't performed, it still happened that we got a trip,' recounts Lars.

Sensible choices

During his early days as a junior player at Randers Freja, Lars completes his final year of primary school at Grønhøjskolen in the village of Øster Terslev. In 1973, the Elstrup family moved from the apartment above the local grocery store to a detached house in Råby, while an elderly couple took over the store apartment. These kind people help Tage with various errands for the store and regularly drive Lars and Peter to their football training in Randers.

After finishing primary school, Lars begins his studies at EFG Trade & Office and later attends two years of business school (HH) at Randers Handelsskole. During this period, he lives with his older cousin Preben and Preben's wife in Randers, which makes it easier for Lars to manage his studies and football training.

Although Lars plays football at a senior level, he still needs a regular job alongside this. His HH diploma qualifies him for a career in the banking sector, and he starts as a banking apprentice at Den Danske Bank in Randers. It is a natural career choice for Lars, who has already shown an interest in work and, a bit later, an ability to save and invest.

At the age of four, Lars sees his father give his employee, a young boy, his wages and say, 'Thank you for your work!' As soon as the boy leaves, little Lars asks Tage, 'Work? What is that, Dad?' Tage is pleased with his son's interest in work and willingness to do something. So, when Lars is old enough, his work enthusiasm is rewarded with a small job at Tage's grocery store. Lars is allowed to sort bottles and restock shelves, but the princely wage of two Danish kroner per hour is not allowed to gather dust or be wasted away.

While Peter goes to the grill bar in Udbyhøj and spends his money there, Lars frequently goes to the local savings bank to deposit his earnings into a savings account or to acquire a bond. So, when Lars moves in with Preben in Randers, he has a self-saved fortune of nearly 40,000 Danish kroner in his account. It's a substantial amount for a 17-year-old in the early part of the decade, characterised by a recession and called the 'poor '80s'.

However, Lars also knows how to spend some of his money wisely on necessary and beneficial things, such as getting a driver's licence. He obtains it when he turns 18, while his preferred vehicle, a red Toyota, is borrowed from his father. Lars will soon make good use of the licence and the car.

But neither money nor success on the football field can erase Lars's fundamental characteristics of insecurity, anxiety, and introversion. These become even more prevalent during his adolescence.

'My teenage years were characterised by insecurity and anxiety,' states Lars. 'If there was a party at school, EFG, HH, or with the football team, the first thing I thought was that I didn't want to go to that party. But I had to go along so as not to seem strange or peculiar when everyone else enjoyed partying.

'When I arrived at a party, the first thing I thought about was when and how I could leave with my dignity intact. I had no desire to drink, play music, shout loudly, or anything. All I thought about was when I could go home. It was always about getting away, away, away, and not showing myself.'

However, on the football field, the young Lars is noticeable, whether he's out on the left wing or in the opponents' penalty area.

Breakthrough and blossoming

Lars's big footballing breakthrough comes in a match against Frederikshavn in November 1982. Randers Freja are engaged in a desperate battle to avoid relegation from the second division. But they regain hope when, in one of the season's last matches, they travel to the northern part of Jutland and secure an impressive

7-1 victory, with 21-year-old Lars contributing two goals and an assist. Despite the victory, the season ends with relegation to the third division. However, the following year, Freja secure a quick return to the second division.

Per Røntved has left the club, but Freja have built a strong young squad consisting of players like Ryan Otkjær, Bo Florin, and the Elstrup brothers. In the autumn of 1985, Randers Freja secure promotion to the top tier.

The promotion happens during one of the most transformative periods in Danish football. While Freja celebrate their spot in the country's top league, Brøndby IF celebrate their first Danish championship and set a course towards full-time professionalism, stock market listing, and international success. In the same autumn, the Danish national team qualifies for the World Cup for the first time. With a national side capable of competing at the highest international level, Danish football develops a new self-awareness.

While the nation goes wild with collective euphoria over the national team's success, honouring heroes like Preben Elkjær and Michael Laudrup, people in Randers and the surrounding area rejoice in having a first division team again. Even during challenging times, the football fans in Randers have shown strong support for Freja, and 4,000 people gather at the city hall to celebrate the local promotion heroes. Perhaps it's a small taste of what Lars will experience seven years later at Rådhuspladsen in Copenhagen.

In 1985, however, the national team is not something Lars contemplates. Yet he has a certain connection to the national team universe on a daily basis. In Randers, he is coached by Austrian Ernst Netuka, who was the Denmark coach in 1967. Netuka leaves a strong impression in Randers. With an infectious spirit, plenty of experience, and a notorious commitment to the development of young players, Netuka often attends youth team matches and training sessions. He is the perfect coach for a team like the current young Freja squad.

'He has managed to create an incredible camaraderie in the club. We are the same players as in previous seasons, but Netuka can make us fight,' says Peter Elstrup to *Ekstra Bladet* on 11 November 1985, after the promotion is secured.

Netuka, who is named Danish Coach of the Year in 1985, understands how to bring out the best in his team, especially in promising talent like Lars. Netuka knows how to alleviate the pressure from his players, understanding that the freer they feel, the better they perform on the field.

One day, team manager Carsten Brandenborg is standing on the sideline with Netuka. Brandenborg has a sceptical expression as he says to his head coach, 'Shouldn't Lars Elstrup run back and do something? He's doing nothing!' To which Netuka calmly replies, 'No, we should leave him alone. Lars can get a chair and sit in the centre circle when we defend.'

That's precisely the approach Lars needs as a footballer and as a person. It is under Netuka at Randers that Lars feels he plays the best football of his career. It is here that he truly feels comfortable, free, and able to perform.

'Ernst Netuka gave me the freedom to play and otherwise left me alone. Just a few short directives, and then I could do as I pleased. That was how he saw me as a player and brought out my potential,' says Lars.

'From the position of left-winger, I could move into the centre, down to the midfield, out to the right wing, or back into the field. And it went well, I blossomed and became the star … maybe.'

Together with Peter, Lars becomes a key figure in the team, and both find the back of the net as promotion is secured with a 5-2 victory over Roskilde. For Lars, it is his 14th goal of the season, a strong contribution that earns him the well-deserved title of Discovery of the Year in the second division of 1985.

The 17 goals are the same as in the previous season, while the first two seasons as a senior yielded seven and 15 goals, respectively.

Naturally, Lars is pleased with the goals, victories, and success. But fundamentally, he loves the play with the ball and enjoys the camaraderie and teamwork within the vibrant Randers team, which never fails to credit their coach for the progress.

When Netuka is confronted with his players' declared love for him after securing promotion, he remarks with a twinkle in his eye, 'That's nice, but I hope they find themselves a sweet girl instead.' But Lars has already found such a girl.

The first time

Throughout the first five years of life as a teenager, 18-year-old Lars was genuinely afraid of even talking to girls. However, on one occasion in middle school, he overcomes his fear of the opposite sex and flirts a little with the class's attractive blonde girl. She is into Lars, who nervously takes note of her beautiful figure. They kiss and touch each other a bit, 'but it never leads to sex … for one reason or another', as Lars puts it.

'At some point, one starts to notice girls to figure out what they are like. And I was very interested in how their bodies looked because I had seen pictures of women,' he says.

'And what is sex? How does it work? It was something I had never heard anyone talk about or discussed with anyone. But the interest was definitely there, and at some point, I also thought about trying to be with a girl.'

Lars's general interest in girls receives a new and specific boost when, still inexperienced, he becomes attracted to his HH classmate Tina.

'She was beautiful, nice, lovely, and pretty. If I were to have a girlfriend, I wanted it to be her,' Lars recalls.

'But at school, I kept my distance from the table where the girls sat. So my best friend and classmate André, who was good at talking to girls, became an intermediary for my contact with her.'

However, Lars had to do the seducing himself. And somewhere inside him, curiosity, desire, and hormones took over from his notorious introversion, shyness, and aversion to youth parties.

'If you were going to interact with a girl, it had to be at a party. That was my approach. One evening, there was a party at school. Tina was going as well, and that was the reason I showed up,' says Lars. 'I had just obtained my driver's licence and arrived at the party by car. At one point, I asked her if she wanted to come with me to Råby. She said yes but also mentioned that she was menstruating. But I didn't care, I said. And I didn't even consider that her menstruation meant she couldn't get pregnant that night. I just wanted to have sex.

'Even if she had been without arms or legs, sick, or needed to vomit, I still wanted her to come with me,' laughs Lars, who later that evening became a man in his own bedroom in Råby.

The experience of intimacy was by no means frightening for Lars. On the contrary.

Girlfriends

Fortunately, the desire and interest are mutual. They enjoy each other's company, and Tina often visits Lars in Råby, while Lars visits her at her parents' house in Mariager.

'I remember that Tina even had a double bed. She had a previous boyfriend, and she told me he had a huge penis. I didn't think mine was particularly big and couldn't understand why she had chosen me as a boyfriend. We never talked about it, though,' he says.

'But we started seeing each other more, also going on trips to her parents' summer house, and it ended up with us moving in together in an apartment on Energivej in Randers. That's when I really moved away from home.'

He experiences a harmonious period as a young man in his early 20s, with a girlfriend, business school, and plenty of football. However, the relationship does not change anything in terms of his personality.

'Having a girlfriend was self-confidence-boosting, and when you had a girlfriend, you weren't completely out of sync with the others. You had experienced something and had something to offer compared to them,' he says.

'But I still didn't feel like going to parties and still thought about how I could escape uncomfortable situations. I still felt insecure, scared, uneasy, and didn't talk to anyone about anything that could alleviate the inner pressure I felt.

'And even though I had a girlfriend, I was still shy and didn't engage in more conversations with a freer mind than before. That didn't change,' Lars emphasises.

A new and completely different girlfriend awaits Lars just ahead. And a new and, in many ways, quite different football life. Far away from home.

4

A Brief Visit to Brøndby

HALF A year before Lars Elstrup is named the Most Promising Player of the Year in the second division, the two suburban rivals from Copenhagen, Hvidovre IF and Brøndby IF, court his favour. The location of the two clubs suits him well, both geographically and as top clubs in the Danish first division.

At Danske Bank, where goalscorer Elstrup is known as banking apprentice Elstrup, they are happy to see newly trained bank assistants seeking new and greater challenges away from familiar surroundings.

'At that time, it was customary for newly trained banking apprentices to be encouraged to seek jobs in a bank branch in a larger city in order to gain experience. I also received such encouragement and was prepared to move to Copenhagen to continue my banking career there,' says Lars.

Thus, it is not the goals on the field or sudden football ambitions that initially lead Lars towards the capital, but rather his civilian career. However, vigilant scouts in the football community have taken note of his achievements on the football field and his civilian career plans.

He is contacted by the charismatic newspaper editor and football official, Niels Erik Madsen, who has shaped the success of Hvidovre IF in recent years, winning the Danish championship in 1981, among other achievements. Around the same time, Lars receives an inquiry from Hvidovre's neighbouring club, Brøndby IF, who, in the summer of 1985, look like serious contenders for the championship. Brøndby's manager, the doctor from Randers, Per Bjerregaard, has in recent years shown a knack for combining football business and association.

The club's sale of talented icon Michael Laudrup to Italian club Lazio in 1983 may have cost them their first championship, but it also gave Brøndby an unprecedented financial dominance in Danish club football. With their wealth, a diligent and dedicated organisation, and Bjerregaard's eye for football talent and human processes, the club has also built a strong understanding of community, ambition, the will to win, and social values.

Brøndby want to be the best, and they want Lars Elstrup.

BIF versus Hvidovre

In the summer of 1985, Lars has meetings with both Madsen and Bjerregaard. 'Serious contract offers' for the young player are on the agenda for both clubs.

'After each of the two meetings, I said I would think about the offer and such. But I was not really in doubt that it should definitely be Brøndby,' Lars explains.

'I instinctively knew that from the meeting with the two individuals, Madsen and Bjerregaard, without saying that one was a better or worse person than the other.

'But I felt more comfortable with Per Bjerregaard. He also had his connection to Randers, which we talked about, and I dared to say some things to him. I listened to him, and he told me what he could help me with. He could be a support for me and provide me with some security, so it ended up with me signing a contract with Brøndby.'

Bjerregaard's empathetic sense also benefits him in recruiting Lars. As a teenager in the early 1960s, Bjerregaard himself had moved from a safe and comfortable football life in Randers to a life in Brøndbyøster's newly built area together with his parents. Upon arrival, he experienced some very difficult years marked by disappointments and loneliness, which were only broken when he became involved in the local club.

For the people's connoisseur Bjerregaard, personal and social security are therefore obvious topics in his conversation with Lars.

Furthermore, Bjerregaard has positive experience in providing jobs for his part-time players. For example, when they easily replaced left-back Kim Christofte, who was sold to Belgian club Lokeren, with national team defender Ole Madsen from Esbjerg FB, in addition to the part-time contract with the club they were able to offer bank assistant Madsen a position in a bank branch in Greve, just a few postal codes away from Brøndby Stadium.

Bjerregaard also manages Lars's job needs in the banking world, this time with the logistical bonus that the young bank assistant gets a job at the Danish Bank's branch at Brøndbyøster Station, a five-minute bus ride from Brøndby Stadium and the training fields that will host the promising football talent from Råby from the beginning of 1986.

'I had already signed a contract with Brøndby during the summer break of '85. However, the contract did not take effect until 1 January 1986, and it is probably the first and only time I have signed a new agreement before the expiration of my current one. Otherwise, I have always waited until the last moment, either just before or just after the expiration of a contract,' says Lars.

'I had four good years as a senior player at Freja and had somehow become a local boy. But people in Randers knew my situation and understood that I needed to move on. It was fully acceptable and legal for me to sign a contract with another club. Nobody thought I was "betraying" Randers Freja by switching to a new and bigger club. No, it was just part of my development, people believed, and I felt good about it.

'So I continued to play amateur football in Randers and went to work at the bank without feeling any pressure that I now had to switch to a new club in the upcoming season.'

And free from pressure – his own or from others – Lars performs brilliantly in the year that is, in many ways, nearly perfect for him. He enjoys every football day at Randers Freja and has sorted out his civilian career and football future. And he has even found a new and lovely girlfriend.

Lolita appears

Three to four months after breaking up with his first girlfriend, Tina, Lars is invited to a party at his team-mates Brian Storvang and Lars Nørregaard's place. As already established, big parties are not Lars's thing, but a fancy dress ball with many of his club-mates tempts him nonetheless. And he decides to wear a very funny costume.

Across from him at the dining table, Lars sees a beautiful young girl whom he is meeting for the first time. During dinner and while simultaneously enjoying several beers, he gathers the courage to address this young lady by her Spanish-sounding name.

'Lolita … Lolita … Lolita,' he whispers mischievously to her. The girl is entirely Danish, but her name is Spanish and means 'little girl'. However, the name association that Lars finds amusing is somewhat different.

'Lolita, yes. I still have trouble pronouncing her name without stumbling over my tongue because back then, people associated that name with a Lolita doll that you could buy in a sex shop if you were a man who wanted to have sex with a plastic doll,' he admits.

'So her name was somewhat scary to me because how could someone be named Lolita? How could any parents think of calling their daughter that? It was completely foreign to me, but she was definitely lovely and attractive.'

Lars continues his occasional 'Lolita' whispers throughout the afternoon and into the evening hours. Not too often, not too infrequent. Just in between.

And occasionally – not too often, not too infrequent – Lolita glances over at the slightly tipsy and peculiar man who sporadically whispers her name with equal parts fascination, absurdity, and interest.

However, the lovely Lolita doesn't see a man's face; she sees an animal costume. At the costume party, Lars, the shy and introverted young man, has dressed up as a gorilla!

'Yes, I wore that gorilla costume the entire evening and sat there for three hours saying her name, "Lolita, Lolita, Lolita!" She just looked at me and said to the others, "Who the hell is he? Who the hell is that clown?" And I sat inside the costume, sweating like a horse. But I didn't dare take it off and show her who I was,' Lars recounts with laughter.

'But at some point, I took off the gorilla head because I had to ask her if she wanted to come home with me to sleep. She agreed, but she made it clear that she only wanted to sleep. But at least it was something to bring a girl home. And at the same time, it would be significant if someone saw me leaving the party with a woman.'

The agreement is upheld. Only sleep occurs, and early the next morning, Lolita takes a taxi home. Despite the slightly bizarre scene, a good and loving chemistry develops between Lolita and Lars, proving to be long-lasting.

'Lolita was lovely, and she still is. She was lively and spirited, attended parties, and could outdrink just about anyone. And I ended up having her as my girlfriend,' says Lars, who now experiences an entirely new type of woman in his life.

'Lolita and Tina were two different girls. While Tina was more of a family-oriented person who wanted domestic cosiness and children, Lolita believed that children were something to be sent out to play on the highway. She sure as hell didn't want children!

'But Lolita and I were also two opposites who came together. What she saw in me might have been the quiet, calm, thoughtful, and organised guy who was skilled in his fields. She was the more outgoing one who raced ahead, and perhaps that's why we were drawn to each other?

'However, we didn't talk about why we were attracted to each other. We didn't get that far.'

Collapse upon arrival

On 1 January 1986, Peter Elstrup and Lolita drive Lars to his new residence in Ordrup, north of Copenhagen. Lars has known for six months that he is moving. He has prepared himself for the dual career change and said goodbye to family and friends. Lars and Lolita are still together, but they have agreed that she should continue her job as a gas station attendant in Egå outside Århus for the time being. The plan is to move in together in Copenhagen at a later time.

Lars's new home is a kind of dormitory where six to eight other bank employees live.

As Lars stands outside the house unloading his belongings, a certain unrest begins to smoulder within him. The unfamiliarity of everything new and the unease of being alone far away from home start to affect him as he carries his things into the building.

Although Lars had already moved out 'part-time' at the age of 17 and a few years later had his own apartment in Randers, this is different. Initially, he lived with his cousin and also had Peter in town. And it only took him 20 minutes to drive home to his parents in Råby and a little longer to visit his sweet grandmother in Udbyhøj. His friends and football team-mates were just around the corner. And the girlfriends, especially. First Tina, then Lolita.

Lars has always been shy and introverted, but never lonely and abandoned because there were always people to meet up with if he felt like it. But now they are all far away, as are the familiar surroundings. And his budding unease only increases when he opens the door to his new home and finds it anything but inviting.

'When I arrived with my few belongings and entered this dormitory, it was incredibly dirty and messy. There were dishes in the sink and all over the tables, and rubbish bags were scattered everywhere,' he recalls.

'There was also not a soul present to talk to. And my room was almost empty. The only things in it were a bed, or rather a cot, and a lamp … without a lampshade.'

After Peter has said goodbye and driven back to Jutland, Lars sits on the cot and looks around at the empty walls in the lonely and charmless room. He thinks of his girlfriend, his friends, his family. His tear ducts have already opened, and he feels a chilling sense of homesickness and abandonment spreading through his nerve pathways.

'I lay in my bed and cried for four consecutive hours. I felt completely alone and lost in the world, thinking, "What am I doing here? What have I gotten myself into?"

'I just didn't feel "big" enough to be in this place where I was. Now I was all alone and didn't have my familiar daily life. I didn't have my team-mates who liked me, with whom I could chat and who could acknowledge the performances I made on the field.

'And I also had my good moments in the locker room, on the training field, in the matches, on bus rides, and in card games where we just laughed and had fun. Suddenly, all of that was gone, and I was in a completely foreign place, all alone.

'I didn't feel like going to work at the bank or playing football,' Lars says and dryly notes, 'but I had to.'

At this point, the entire new life in the capital seems so overwhelmingly daunting that it's surprising he can even gather himself on the following day. Get up and off to his new job and then to the new football club.

'I cried myself to sleep that night,' says Lars. 'But I knew I had to get up and go to work the next morning. I knew I had to put on some clothes, have breakfast, and figure out how the S-train worked so I could get from Ordrup to Brøndbyøster Station.'

I knew I had to meet my boss and my new colleagues wearing a shirt, tie, and nice trousers, which I hated wearing. I knew I had to start doing some banking work and play football. I knew that everyday life had to continue.

'But when I look back, 1 January 1986 was the day when I was the saddest in my entire life,' Lars concludes about the day that also happened to be his first as a paid football player.

Among Danish champions

Despite homesickness and that initial breakdown, Lars gets off to a good start at Brøndby IF. He has been recruited to the club as a replacement for the popular striker Anders Sundstrup, who is set to move to French club FC Sochaux in the upcoming summer break. Until then, Lars will compete with Sundstrup, two years his senior; another former Netherlands professional, Tommy Christensen; and the small top scorer Claus Nielsen for the two available attacking positions in coach Ebbe Skovdahl's regular 4-4-2 formation.

The competition is tough, but the camaraderie is top-notch. Lars quickly becomes part of the colourful but social squad of the reigning Danish champions, which also includes iconic Brøndby defenders like record appearance-maker Bjarne Jensen and the giant John Widell, goalkeeper Ole Nørrevang, midfielders Henrik Jensen and John Helt, as well as his future national team colleagues, midfield workhorse John 'Faxe' Jensen and captain and defensive conductor Lars Olsen.

'I was very well received, and I have only positive memories of the camaraderie and the atmosphere in the club, which appealed to me tremendously,' Lars says about his arrival at Brøndby.

'And I actually felt quite comfortable being among the players who were the Danish champions. They were the best players in Denmark, the ones who were the big stars, the ones who were your idols, the ones who were more skilled and better than oneself, and suddenly I was among them.

'But I loved going to training and playing together with these guys and somehow managed to fit in among them.'

He can do so right from the first training matches in January and February 1986, where Lars shows that he is worth investing in. He scores a total of seven goals leading up to the start of the season in early spring, and it is clear that Brøndby's attacking style suits him quite well. 'Aerial play is not my strong suit, but in Brøndby, we play fluid combination play on the ground, and it gives me many opportunities,' he confidently tells *Ekstra Bladet* before the start of the new season.

He is proven right. When the season begins, he shows that he can score goals even though the matches now take place in the top league in the country. He scores the winning goal with a decisive half-volley away against Ikast, but Lars takes the success in his usual modest style. 'Of course, it's nice to score the winning goal, but for me, there's more to football than just scoring goals,' he states after the match, where he self-critically notes to *Ekstra Bladet* on 7 April, 'I had a hard time shaking off Stefan Gerbert's tight marking, and that probably has something to do with getting used to the faster pace in the first division.'

However, it is a pace that Lars gets the opportunity to adapt to full-time. His debut in the first division coincides with Brøndby becoming the first Danish club to introduce full-time professionalism. At that time, it was a bold and risky step, but according to the innovative chairman Per Bjerregaard, it was the only way for Danish football to develop internationally. The ambition at Brøndby was no longer just to reclaim the championship but also to go far in the European Cup, in which the club would participate for the first time in the autumn of 1986.

This marked a definite paradigm shift in Danish club football, especially for the involved Brøndby players. Full-time professionalism and international ambitions inevitably brought higher expectations, increased media exposure, higher performance demands, and intensified competition within the team. But that didn't scare the otherwise modestly ambitious football boy from Råby. The prospect of becoming a full-time professional suited Lars more than just well.

Win/win

Professionalism at Brøndby meant that all players in the first team were offered full-time contracts starting from 1 March 1986.

'The club offered me the salary I received at Danske Bank plus the salary I already had from my part-time contract. It meant that I would have a salary of 19,500 kroner gross plus various bonuses. The salary wasn't impressive, but the opportunity to make a living from my hobby was a welcome chance for me and many of the players who struggled to make ends meet with family, job, training, and matches,' says Lars.

'And when Per Bjerregaard presented me with the offer and asked if the club could buy me out from the bank, I said "yes, please", without hesitation and gladly.'

For Lars, the offer of a full-time contract was also a welcome opportunity to escape the mundane everyday life at the bank, where he felt like a 'caged hen in a tie'. It didn't help that his colleagues weren't really interested in football. They had a hard time understanding why he needed time off for training and matches. Most of them also sensed that Lars didn't really enjoy his life as a bank assistant.

'My passion had always been football and the joy and playfulness of the sport. And now I could make money and be a professional football player, even a full-time professional, have the rest of the time off, and not think about anything else but playing football,' says Lars, who quickly moves from the mess and loneliness in the Ordrup dormitory to a villa in nearby Hellerup, where he lives for a few months. Although the windows shake when the S-train passes by, this new home provides Lars with a safer, more social, and positive everyday life.

'I lived there with three other Jutland bank assistants. Good friends who were there when you came home, and we cooked together. They were wonderful people, while in Ordrup, I had hardly met anyone because they probably didn't want to be there in the mess,' says Lars, who with his full-time contract decides to move in together with Lolita.

They find a townhouse in Greve, south of Copenhagen, where they become neighbours with Tommy Christensen and his girlfriend Gitte, who also become part of the social community. Lars looks up to Tommy, a former professional player with Spanish club Elche CF, Dutch team PSV Eindhoven, and Leicester City and Portsmouth in England. Occasionally, Lars accompanies him when he takes his German Shepherd for a walk.

It is springtime in Denmark and springtime for Lars. In the bright months of 1986, he experiences a really good time with his girlfriend, football, and strong social bonds. A stark contrast to the setback that greeted him in the almost empty room in Ordrup on the first day of the year.

Lars recalls, 'In Brøndby, I got close to Bjarne Jensen and his girlfriend Mette, whom Lolita and I visited at home. And especially to John Helt, who was a central figure in the team and a pleasant person. I also liked Henrik Jensen, but I liked them all. There was no one in the team who made me feel uneasy or uncomfortable. Rather the opposite.'

Full-time football

But work needs to be done and performance needs to be delivered, in training and on matchdays. The man in charge of the first group of Danish full-time professionals is the carpenter-trained

Ebbe Skovdahl, who later gets to manage both Portuguese giants Benfica and Scottish club Aberdeen. He is also the uncle of Michael and Brian Laudrup, but Skovdahl's own football talent has a different character than that of his nephews. As a player, Skovdahl is known as a tough fighter and motivator, especially during his time on Brøndby's Danmarksserie and third division teams in the early 1970s.

Skovdahl has a direct but down-to-earth approach to his players. And he has a clear playing concept for them. Skovdahl particularly emphasises his players' physical fitness as full-time professionals. It should be used to press the opponents' ball carrier all over the field throughout the game, which also involves specific defensive and physical tasks for the team's attacking players like Lars.

'Compared to Ernst Netuka in Randers, Ebbe Skovdahl was a different coach,' says Lars after a moment's thought.

'With Ebbe in Brøndby, there were tactical meetings and an introduction to the new playing system, 4-4-2. He told us very clearly how we should move in relation to each other, how I should press as a striker and fulfil my role. Something that I naturally tried to do when the coach wanted it and we were setting up a team tactic. And of course, you listen to what the coach says.

'But I also didn't have any fear or anything when it came to Ebbe. Not that I talked to him much, but somehow he let me be and had a good understanding of who I was, just like my team-mates did.'

Football is different, but it remains a pleasure for full-time professional Lars, who truly experiences the contrast between professionals and amateurs when he and Brøndby crush the newly promoted Randers Freja 5-0 at Brøndby Stadium.

In the encounter between the present and the past, Lars scores once, while his older brother Peter in the Freja jersey has to settle for a consolation hug after the match.

However, the competition for attacking positions is fierce, and Lars has to get used to a new role as a true centre-forward instead of his usual position as a left-winger. In his seven league matches, Lars finds the net twice and is performing well in the squad that is on the expected course to defend the national title.

But the spring season of 1986 is shortened due to the World Cup finals in Mexico and the national team's preparations in May.

Lars enjoys a carefree summer holiday and follows the World Cup on TV.

In a couple of unforgettable weeks in June, Denmark defeat Scotland, Uruguay, and West Germany in succession, and look like definite World Cup contenders. The country is in a national football ecstasy, but Lars also looks ahead to his own tasks on the football field. First and foremost, the Intertoto Cup matches of the summer.

Interest from Feyenoord

Originally, the UEFA Intertoto Cup was created to provide European football enthusiasts with some matches to bet on during the summer break. However, it also serves as a warm-up for clubs ahead of their new season. It is Brøndby IF's fourth consecutive participation, but this summer, the Intertoto matches are particularly important as preparation for the club's first ties in the European Cup in September.

With Anders Sundstrup gone, there is one fewer competitor, and Lars starts in the first Intertoto match against the Polish team Widzew Łódź at home. He is ready; it only takes him eight minutes to put Brøndby ahead. After just over an hour he doubles the lead, and two minutes before the end he sets up Henrik Jensen's final goal, making it 3-0.

The day before, Denmark had defeated West Germany 2-0 and won Group E in the World Cup. The nation is ecstatic, and Danish football fans enjoy the day after with match reports, media coverage, and joyous celebrations.

The Intertoto Cup tie between Brøndby and Widzew Łódź on Saturday, 18 June 1986 is a modest affair. It takes place on one of the training pitches at Brøndby Stadium, and only 358 spectators attend. Among them are representatives from the Dutch powerhouse club Feyenoord, including the Dutchman Peter Stefan, a football agent, former manager at the Rotterdam club, and a close partner of Per Bjerregaard and Brøndby. The rumour quickly spreads; it is the second time that Feyenoord have seen Lars play. The club is in need of a central striker and now believes that Elstrup is the right man for the job.

Out in the car park behind the field, Lars is putting his football boots in the car when his neighbour, team-mate, and Dutch-speaking Tommy Christensen approaches him with a smile and an interesting piece of information.

'He told me that there were people from Feyenoord who wanted to buy me. I couldn't understand it, and I didn't believe it. I just needed to go home and take a shower,' says Lars.

But things are moving quickly now.

Four years earlier, Brøndby allied themselves with Stefan, who familiarises Per Bjerregaard with both the written and unwritten rules of the football transfer market. During one of their first player sales, Brøndby voluntarily gave Stefan a generous bonus, and this calculated conduct proves to be a golden investment. Stefan generously shares his knowledge, and the talented Bjerregaard absorbs it. He skilfully manages acquisitions and talent development for resale, turning it into a core business that improves the club's finances. This financial leeway ensures a continuous quality in the team, where good players can be replaced by equally good players.

Something that now has to work in favour of the football-talented and money-minded Lars.

The millionaire dream

A couple of days after Lars's successful match against Widzew Łódź, Stefan and representatives from Feyenoord are set to negotiate with Bjerregaard. He has proven himself a skilled negotiator several times before, both for 'his' players and for Brøndby. Before the meeting with the Dutch, Bjerregaard and Lars have a conversation in Brøndby's clubhouse.

'Per Bjerregaard thought it was too early for me to sign a contract with a foreign club. He saw Olympic national team potential in me and believed that I needed to further develop my football skills. He could also see the bigger picture because if I were sold as an Olympic national team player, both the club and I could earn more money. So, in that way, he was looking out for both his and my best interests,' says Lars.

'And yes, he actually advised me to wait, and I heard him well, but still, I thought, "No, I need to sign the contract now!" I would rather have a million kroner in my hand now than not get anything if I were never sold. Money was at the forefront, and it weighed more in my considerations than whether this was the right or wrong club choice.

'You never know what will happen when you make a decision in your life. That can only be seen with hindsight, and when I look at it, it was a decision made to become a millionaire and embark on an adventure again. That's how I saw it, and when you have that mindset, the future can turn out the way you want it.'

With Lars's authorisation, Brøndby's chairman then negotiates with the Dutch while the player waits in a separate room.

'After the clubs had negotiated for some time, Per Bjerregaard came out to me and told me what the Dutch were willing to offer in terms of monthly salary and that they would provide a car, rented accommodation, and other things for me. "Are you satisfied with that?" he asked. "Yes, I damn well am," I thought, but at the same time, it would be nice to get a little more. So, I said, "Naaah, I would like a bit more. What about an extra 50,000 kroner?"

'Then he went back to the meeting room, came out with an increased offer, and asked again, "Are you satisfied now?" And I didn't dare push it further, so I just signed the contract.'

The Dutch end up paying Lars an amount of nearly one million kroner as a transfer fee and a monthly salary of 14,000 kroner, plus various bonuses and benefits. The amount is lower than what he received at Brøndby and significantly less compared to the salaries top players receive today. However, with the lower Dutch tax, Lars ends up receiving a larger amount than as a full-time professional at Brøndby.

It seems like a big leap to go from the fledgling full-time Brøndby to Rotterdam and the established powerhouse of Feyenoord. In any case, it is considerably larger than the journey from Randers to the capital half a year earlier. And this time, the preparation is much shorter.

The day after the negotiations in Brøndby's clubhouse and four days after the Łódź match, Lars is on a plane heading to the Netherlands, where he will immediately join Feyenoord's pre-season training camp.

Denmark's World Cup dream has just been shattered by a stinging 5-1 defeat to Spain, and like all other Danes, Lars is disappointed with the ruthless exit. But more than anything, he is a young man looking straight into a hopeful future in a new country and at a powerhouse club. With a million in his bank account, a sponsored car in the garage, and the lovely and adventurous Lolita by his side.

5

Hell in the Netherlands

THE RELOCATION to Rotterdam is not particularly difficult for Lars. Instead of a shabby room in a filthy dormitory, he is greeted with a cosy townhouse in the suburb of Dordrecht, 10 miles from Rotterdam. Rotterdam itself is a blend of 1950s concrete buildings and bold and modern 1980s architecture, earning the historic port city on the Maas River the nickname 'Manhattan on the Maas'. The Dutch version of New York City, if you will.

For village boy Lars, Dordrecht serves as a fine and peaceful oasis away from the bustling centre of Rotterdam.

'It was actually easier to move from Copenhagen to Holland than it was to move from Randers to Copenhagen. I had grown a bit older and also had Lolita with me,' says Lars, who approached his new world with an open mind.

'As a 23-year-old, it was exciting to come to Dordrecht and Rotterdam. New places where people spoke a different language, the buildings looked different, and there were interesting things to see. Plenty of canals, cafes, and city life.'

As he has already discovered, Lolita is a lover of life. Her indulgence in life's pleasures is significant. She enjoys parties and going out, and in that regard, Dordrecht and Rotterdam are a perfect fit for the lively Lolita, whom her former mother-in-law remembers as 'really sweet but quite unique and quite a pleasure seeker, I must say'.

However, the domestically skilled Ingelise Elstrup is not impressed by her daughter-in-law's household skills.

'It was Lars who cooked all the meals, did the laundry, and so on because he liked to live in a tidy place. She didn't do much at home,' notes Ingelise.

Despite their obvious differences, it's nice for Lars to have his girlfriend's company in the foreign land. Their relationship is going well, and the first three months at the football club are primarily a pleasure. But as autumn approaches, darkness also descends upon Lars's mind.

The encounter with Feyenoord

In Feyenoord, Lars joins a prestigious and successful club. Founded back in 1908, it has 12 national championships, six cup triumphs, and two European competition wins, adding a third in the decades after Lars's years with the club. A fanatical following of up to 50,000 people fills De Kuip ('The Tub'), demanding dedicated effort. These fans remember how the club, two years before Elstrup's arrival, won both the championship and the cup in the 1983/84 season with Johan Cruyff and Ruud Gullit on the team. Cruyff, a legendary figure, spent his last season in the Eredivisie as a successful protest action against his old club and notorious Feyenoord rivals, Ajax, who refused to offer him a final contract.

Cruyff's revenge was fulfilled and it was also his last year on the football field. However, it is considered a minor catastrophe that Feyenoord have finished third in the past two seasons, with Ajax and other rivals PSV Eindhoven taking the titles.

The self-perception at Feyenoord is set in stone, and the expectations of new victories and successful experiences animate, motivate, or hang as a burden over the current Feyenoord players, depending on their temperament and mental resources.

Feyenoord is also a club with a tradition of having Danes on the team. In the 1970s, the 'Wizard' Jørgen Kristensen dazzled on the wing, and shortly before Lars's arrival they parted ways with defender Ivan Nielsen, midfielder Jan Sørensen, and goalscorer John Eriksen. The latter scored 22 goals in 33 matches in the previous season, and there are increased expectations for Lars as the next Danish goal machine in the Feyenoord jersey.

From the beginning, Lars occupies the central position as a striker in a classic Dutch three-man attack, which often includes the small dribbler Regi Blinker who will later go on to play for Celtic and Sheffield Wednesday, and the future Feyenoord coach, Mario Been, on the flanks. It is a system that Lars is familiar with from his left-wing position at Randers, and already in the friendly matches he shows that he can adapt to the higher Dutch level. He scores plenty of goals in the friendlies and even scores on his league debut against Zwolle.

Team-mates, fans, and the Dutch press are impressed by the Danish acquisition, whom no one knew before. Critical voices have even claimed that an 'unknown Danish attacker' would hardly be able to strengthen a top Dutch team like Feyenoord. But Lars proves them wrong as he quickly starts performing. Fellow countryman and left-back Jan Heintze, who plays for PSV Eindhoven, is impressed by Lars and states to *Ekstra Bladet* after his debut match, 'Incredibly positive things are being written about Elstrup. He has impressed everyone in a short period of time, and after watching him in action on TV, I understand why.'

However, Lars's success lasts only a couple of weeks. Then his performances on the field begin to fluctuate, and the goals dry up. After five months at the club, with a measly three goals to his name, he starts receiving massive criticism from both fans and the local press. It culminates in a disappointing performance as Feyenoord definitively say goodbye to the championship with a goalless match at Zwolle. After the game, the Dutch newspaper *Algemeine Dagblad* writes, 'The Dane truly works for the team and gives it his all. But he was signed to score goals, and he's not doing that. That's why many are after his scalp. When things don't work in a team, there's always a need to find scapegoats.'

And the finger increasingly points towards Lars Elstrup.

The decline begins

Lars hasn't become a worse football player since his arrival in Rotterdam, but mentally, it becomes more challenging for him to perform. 'I'm a person who needs security and trust from the coach to thrive and perform. And that was lacking in Holland,' he says today.

Trust, something he received in different ways under Ernst Netuka at Randers and Ebbe Skovdahl at Brøndby. But Lars's coach at Feyenoord is neither Netuka nor Skovdahl, but Rinus Israel. As a player, he was known as 'Iron Rinus' due to his tough playing style in the centre of Feyenoord's defence. He was the obvious team captain and led Feyenoord to several triumphs both domestically and internationally throughout 12 seasons, culminating in victory in the 1970 European Cup Final, where they became the first Dutch club to win a European trophy. He was also part of the Dutch national team that reached the World Cup Final in 1974.

As a coach, he is not much different from his playing days. He is tough and a winner. He demands discipline from his players, leaving no room for individual freedom. Defeats are also mercilessly and immediately punished.

'If we lost a match on Sunday, we knew that the first half-hour of training on Monday would be spent on sliding tackles. Not to improve our tackling skills, but as pure punishment or a form of revenge from the coach,' says Lars.

'What you need after physical and mental exertion is recovery. To regain your strength and energy. So the next day, we should have received massages, warm baths, and loosening up our bodies. Instead, we were subjected to physical training!

'You can shake your head or laugh at it, but if you said so much as a peep to the coach, you would be dropped from the team, kicked out of the squad, or asked to leave the club.

'In such a situation, you feel helpless. And it's not good for your wellbeing to function under a leader whose views clash radically with your own beliefs. But what do you do when you're 23 years old, in a new country, a new club, and you have things to learn? I chose not to say anything.

'And from there, it slowly but steadily went downhill. The first three months were good, but the rest of my time in Holland was a big decline. I became sad, depressed, and more introverted, withdrawing into my own world. I lost my joy for the game and couldn't perform to the expectations and demands I and others had for me.

'And it became an unsolvable situation,' says Lars about the dilemma that increasingly haunts him during his seven-year career as a professional: the internal conflict between his inner desires and self-expression. A life of chronic compromise.

'Iron Rinus' in action

In Lars's first season, Feyenoord players get plenty of practice in sliding tackles because there are many defeats. And when the results begin to falter, and Lars's goals dry up, Rinus Israel directs his criticism towards the Danish forward. In the press, he often states that things could be different if Lars would score some goals. That's Israel's interpretation. And it's the head coach of a prestigious club speaking. Unambiguously. That's the unforgiving demand of the top professional football world. The world that seemed like a pure adventure during Lars's dreams of millions in the townhouse in Greve and in Brøndby's clubhouse. Now he receives harsh blows and his confidence is affected. A vicious cycle is set in motion.

But other players also suffer from Iron Rinus's wrath. Lars's attacking partner, Regi Blinker, will later have a long and distinguished career with Feyenoord, but at this time he is a young kid playing his first senior year. However, that doesn't stop him from dribbling past everyone in training.

'He was only 17 years old when I joined the club, but one of the most talented dribblers I've ever seen. He could do the most incredible things with the ball,' recalls Lars, who has seen coaches give good advice and the occasional scolding in Denmark. But he has never seen a coach come close to doing what Israel does to discipline Blinker's dribbling skills.

It happens in one of the first training sessions that Lars participates in. The players are divided into two teams, and Blinker dribbles around as if the ball is glued to his feet. Despite being 44 years old, Israel actively participates in the training session as if it's a matter of life and death. The same goes for when Blinker comes dribbling towards him. Lars can't believe his eyes when Iron Rinus lets the ball go and launches himself through the air, both legs stretched out and his studs first, to torpedo poor Blinker on his shinbone. Screaming in pain, the young winger falls to the ground, but Israel shows no mercy. The suffering Blinker is ordered to get up so the game can continue.

Lars is shocked, but it won't be the last time he sees the coach subject Blinker to such treatment.

'I vividly remember how Israel kicked Blinker down multiple times during training to toughen him up and prepare him for the treatment he would face in matches,' he says.

Although Lars himself is not a victim of the coach's tackles like Blinker, he is frightened and disgusted by the coach's methods.

'For some players, that kind of treatment might work, but for me, it had the opposite effect. I became afraid of making mistakes and couldn't perform as well, neither in training nor in matches,' he adds.

Blinker also remembers Israel's training methods but has a more relaxed view of them today.

'Feyenoord is a challenging club to play for. And for new players, it requires some adjustment to that kind of training and methods, as Lars experienced. There's nothing strange about it. Many struggle to adapt to Feyenoord, especially foreign players. In that aspect, I don't think Lars was much different from others,' says Blinker.

However, Lars proves to be somewhat 'different'.

Team spirit – the Dutch way

It's not only the coach and training methods that trouble Lars. He also doesn't feel comfortable with the different Dutch approach to team spirit.

'In Denmark, you're team-mates and maybe even friends. In Holland, you're primarily competitors,' he says.

'It was entirely different from what I had been accustomed to, especially in Randers but also in Brøndby.'

In the fully professional Netherlands, football is not played for fun. A significant portion of each player's salary is tied to bonus schemes. Simply put, you earn more if you play instead of sitting on the bench. Therefore, there is fierce competition to be among the coach's chosen ones.

It's a competitive mentality that allows Lars to engage in a friendly game of tennis with his attacking partner Mario Been one day and then be criticised harshly by the same Been during training the next day.

The natural carriers of the culture within the team are the native Feyenoord players: goalkeeper Joop Hiele and defender Sjaak Troost. They set the agenda and ensure that training always takes place in a competitive, sometimes almost hostile manner.

At the beginning, Lars approaches training without being particularly impressed. One of the unwritten rules on the training ground is that you go harder against players lower in the hierarchy than those higher up. However, hierarchy is not something Lars pays much attention to. So, when Troost holds on to the ball a bit too long, the Dane goes in with a tough but fair tackle, winning the ball. Troost lies on the grass for a moment, writhing before getting up, mumbling, and purposefully walking towards Lars. The Dutch defender has murder in his eyes as he coldly says, 'I'll make sure you don't play on Sunday.'

The threat that Troost presents is one that Lars takes seriously, especially when Troost immediately involves Hiele in his intended revenge.

Lars recounts his successful 'rescue mission', 'Then I know their mission is to "get" me. That opportunity arises shortly after when a cross from the right is heading straight towards me. I see out of the corner of my eye Joop Hiele charging towards me, and I sense Troost ready to make a far-from-fair tackle. Fortunately, I time my jump perfectly, smashing the ball into the net while Hiele and Troost collide with each other.'

However, there are other times when he doesn't get off so lightly.

'When I ran towards the ball in training, I could always be sure that an elbow would come flying. Often, players would deliberately hit and kick each other,' says Lars.

Furthermore, his relationship with team-mates isn't all that great. He is willing to play a game of pool or tennis with the other players, but he never truly becomes part of the community.

'Lars Elstrup's relationship with the rest of us wasn't particularly close. He kept to himself, didn't say much, and wasn't very open. He seemed like a nice guy, but he was challenging to get close to,' says Blinker.

'I was also young compared to Lars at the time, and there were cultural differences as he was Danish and I was Dutch. We worked together because we had a common goal, but that was it.'

During the winter of 1986/87, there is nothing to suggest that Lars is breaking out of his familiar shell. On the contrary; he is closing himself off from the outside world at Feyenoord.

Lars also struggles tactically. While the Netherlands is known for promoting offensive football, Feyenoord play with a disciplined and structured style that leaves no room for the individual freedom that benefited Elstrup as a player – and his previous teams.

'In Feyenoord, it was a rule that if you lost the ball in an attack, you had to immediately return to a defensive position. You had to run in fixed ways, defend in fixed ways, and nothing could be slacked off. It was more like "shut up, march, and follow orders" as directed by the coach,' he says.

'But I needed the freedom to do my own creative things and what I thought was best for the team. That's how I functioned best and became productive, constructive, and creative. I scored and assisted goals, played good matches, created entertainment and enjoyable football, and produced results.'

As Lars's freedom is limited in Feyenoord, he becomes stiff in his ball control and loses the intuitive sense of the game, which had been his strength. The fundamental joy of playing football is also reflected in the loss column, and Lars is plagued by increasing performance anxiety.

And the melancholy is not just a momentary occurrence. It lasts for most of his first season at Feyenoord and escalates further in the next.

By the end of his second season at Feyenoord in 1987/88, Lars's sole focus is on getting through the days relatively unscathed. He is now so afraid and filled with anxiety that it has manifested physically. He feels nauseous when he gets into his car to drive to training. And during training, he finds himself in a mental daze that is also noticed by his bewildered team-mates.

'I remember how, on one of the last training days, I was so mentally absent that I was practically running around in a fog,' he says.

'We had to run three laps around the field. I didn't dare to look to the sides or talk to any of the other players. The only thing I thought about was going home and hiding on my sofa.

'I could see the others like Hiele, Troost, Been, and Simon Tahamata, the big star and national team player, running a bit ahead of me. I could sense that they were talking about me and my condition, but I didn't dare speak to anyone and pretended nothing was wrong.

'At one point, Simon Tahamata slows down to come alongside me. Suddenly, he shoulder-checks me, sending me two metres to the side. "See what I mean?" he says afterwards.'

Lars pretends as if nothing happened, but he can see what Tahamata means, and he understands him. He is completely absent. And this is from a team that relies on unity to function. But Lars can't do anything about it. However much he wants to thrive, be successful, and build a good relationship with his team-mates, he can't handle it. All he can think about is getting away. Completely away. Away from the Netherlands, away from Feyenoord, away from Rinus Israel and his constant acts of punishment, away from the hostile competition at training. Away from the life of a professional football player. Away.

The downward spiral seems to have no end in sight. Off the field, the relationship with the rebellious Lolita is crumbling, and Lars decides to end it. It is a decision that is not necessarily easy but largely a consequence of his mental issues.

'I felt that things became overwhelming for me, and there were some unsatisfactory aspects in the relationship,' says Lars. 'Therefore, I had to make the decision that would allow me to find my space and my place again. And that was to end our romantic relationship.'

The break-up with Lolita naturally leaves Lars feeling lonely in his Dutch townhouse, but fortunately, the separation is not aggressive or hostile in nature.

Aggression and hatred, however, are elements he experiences from spectators during several tournament matches where he already struggles with his fragile mental state.

In the late 1980s, Danish fan culture is characterised by a festive, colourful, and peaceful 'support base' that emerged during the national team's successful European Championship and World Cup campaigns in 1984 and 1986. Dutch national team supporters have a similar mentality, but in Netherlands club football, physical intimidation and organised violence have long been integrated into fan culture. This is particularly true at Feyenoord and even at smaller clubs like the infamous ADO Den Haag.

At the intimate Zuiderpark Stadium, the atmosphere among Den Haag's hardcore fans is notoriously hostile, with the players on the field being in close proximity, making it intimidating for away players to take throw-ins or corners. Verbal abuse is one thing, but Lars experiences something far worse during a corner kick in a match at Zuiderpark.

'I walk out to the corner flag and get ready to take the kick,' he recalls. 'Suddenly, out of the corner of my eye, I see something flying through the air. It is heading straight for my head, but I manage to duck and narrowly avoid what turns out to be a rolled-up umbrella!'

The umbrella attack is a more extreme example. More commonly, players at Zuiderpark and other menacing venues have to endure projectiles like coins, lighters, or cans from the crowd.

Lars's parents also have first-hand experience of the extreme Dutch fan culture. When Tage and Ingelise, accompanied by a couple of friends, travel to Amsterdam to attend the heated match between Ajax and Feyenoord, they witness a bus slowly manoeuvring through the busy traffic near Ajax's home stadium.

It turns out to be Feyenoord's team bus. Suddenly, hundreds of Ajax fans rush from various side streets, launching stones at the bus windows and shouting words that can hardly be understood as anything other than a message that Feyenoord's players are unwelcome. Tage, Ingelise, and their friends sit in their car nearby, observing the scene in shock and disbelief.

It is a frightening experience for them, but also for Lars himself, sitting on the bus and witnessing the scenario of rage, aggression, and hatred. He finds it difficult to understand the mentality, the hatred, and the violence. However, the most terrifying experience for Elstrup comes from Feyenoord's own fans.

Feyenoord's fan group, Het Legioen, is among the most loyal in the Netherlands. However, during the rise of hooliganism in Europe, Feyenoord also face problems with violent fan factions. These are individuals who do not let minor details like victories on the pitch prevent them from resorting to violence and vandalism. In the autumn of 1987, for example, Feyenoord play a European match away against Aberdeen, winning a hard-fought game 2-1 (including a goal scored by Elstrup, who still manages to display one of his strengths: penalty execution). Before and after the match, several hundred Feyenoord fans manage to smash all the seats and tables on a charter flight as well as the interiors of several local pubs.

The most extreme fan faction is known as Don't Run Away, and it is likely representatives of this group who decide to send a 'message' to the Danish forward before the last home match of the season against Den Bosch.

Threats

It has been a disappointing season. Not only have Feyenoord been far from the title race, but they finish sixth in the league, missing out on European qualification. Feyenoord's fans are furious, and to rub salt in the wound, main rivals Ajax and PSV have reached the finals of European competitions.

However, what weighs on Lars as he settles into bed in the upstairs bedroom of his townhouse in Dordrecht the day before the final match is the relief of knowing that the season will soon be over. Additionally, his contract with Feyenoord is expiring, and he looks forward to taking a holiday and getting away from it all.

He has struggled through the past few weeks of training and matches. Now there is only one game left, and it will all be over.

However, something suddenly happens in the middle of the night. With a loud crash, two large stones shatter his windows. Lars doesn't have time to see who threw them, but he wakes up to the sound of the shattering glass, takes note of the damage, and returns to bed shaken. The next morning brings another frightening episode as he walks to his car to drive to the match.

He recalls, 'When I get to my car, I see that all four tyres have been slashed. In the window, I find a note with the message, "If you don't start playing better, we will use even harsher methods!"'

It is unknown if other Feyenoord players received the same treatment, but they don't appear particularly motivated as the final match kicks off. Feyenoord lose 4-1 to Den Bosch. Lars experiences being substituted on and soon back off again and, in total, only gets a meagre 15 minutes of playing time.

The fans are furious. One point in the last six games is a catastrophe for a club of Feyenoord's calibre, and the players are booed off the field. However, what terrifies Lars even more is that the fans have travelled all the way to Dordrecht to threaten him.

'At that moment, I knew that if I were to continue living in Holland, it would have to be in an apartment with security guards because I couldn't live with this,' he says.

The same could be said about his life over the past two years – it had become unbearable. Yet, despite the immense mental strain, Lars feels an urgent need to meet the demands and expectations of others rather than interpreting his own inner signals.

However, in the summer of 1988, he manages – apparently – to navigate through what can be described as the tunnel of compromise.

Home to Denmark

Lars never finds out if the fan faction Don't Run Away intends to follow through with their threats because he is quickly on his way out. The Den Bosch match is witnessed by Odense Boldklub's director, Knud Engedahl, who has made the trip to Rotterdam by car with his wife, Mitzi.

'When I meet Knud and Mitzi at a local Greek restaurant after the match, he quickly makes it clear that they would very much like to sign a contract with me,' Lars recalls. Feeling suspicious, he asks, 'Even after what you've seen today?' Engedahl replies, 'Yes, even after what we've seen today.'

However, OB are not the only Danish club interested in Lars. Ikast FS (half of the current FC Midtjylland) are also interested, and his former club Randers Freja seriously consider bringing him back, even though finances are tight. But eight games into the season, Randers Freja are fighting relegation and could benefit from his goalscoring abilities. The interest in Lars is so high that forces within and around Freja organise a fundraising campaign to secure the funds needed to bring the 'lost son' back. On and off the field, Lars has left a highly positive impression in Randers, which even his short stint at Brøndby and two difficult years in the Netherlands hasn't changed.

Despite the fundraising efforts and extensive lobbying, Randers Freja lack the necessary funds to make a serious contract offer. Lars even considers staying in the Netherlands. Yet, despite his lack of success, Feyenoord show an interest in extending his contract. This even happens at the initiative of Rinus Israel, who has been a sharp critic of Lars. But perhaps the coach has 'seen' what Lars himself senses: that he still has something to prove and more goals in him than he has scored so far.

Although his time at Feyenoord hasn't been good, and he longs for home in many ways, something makes him briefly consider the possibility of an extension. He hasn't performed, and that gives him a feeling of having something to prove. Feyenoord's fans haven't truly seen what he is capable of, and that disappoints him. It is the first time he hasn't lived up to expectations, and it feels unsatisfying to leave such a negative impression. Both he and the team can achieve more than they have shown in the past season.

'If the club doesn't bring in new players who are obvious candidates to take my position, they will get my signature. We are a better team than we have shown this year, and I want to be part of proving that,' Lars states to *Ekstra Bladet* in May 1988, as his contract expiration date approaches.

In the end, the desire for security and the prospect of rediscovering his love for the game outweigh the chance to prove his worth and repair his reputation. He signs a contract with OB, effective from the summer of 1988. Lars's career at Feyenoord and two extremely challenging years in the Netherlands are over.

When he looks back at his time in Rotterdam, he also realises that his struggle was more about his own personal issues than the behaviour of the Dutch. Reflecting on it, he says, 'I had a tough time in Holland. But even though the Dutch football culture was different in many ways, and I didn't thrive with the coach's mentality, the biggest problem wasn't the Dutch but the fact that I had personal difficulties. At another time, when I might have been in a better place, I might have found it easier to handle the differences in football culture.'

However, the state of mind – 'having a tough time with oneself' – proves to be a recurring issue for Lars behind the facade of calculated life happiness that is typically projected on to a professional football player.

He is not someone who shares his problems, not even with his parents, who, back home in Råby, are blissfully unaware of their son's struggles. Understandably, they are proud of their boy, and in the small local community, they boast about 'the town's son' being a professional abroad. It is common for Tage, the grocer, to be asked how Lars is doing in the Netherlands, and both he and Ingelise can assure others that he is doing fine. At this time the internet does not yet exist, and there is limited media coverage of a relatively unknown Danish player trying to break through abroad – someone who isn't even close to the national team.

So, in the summer of 1988, outwardly, he is Lars Elstrup, the promising professional football player with great potential, someone whom others rightfully expect something from. Now, back home at OB, they believe they have acquired a matured and sharpened player with experience from top-level foreign football and a knack for scoring goals.

6

Falling in Love With Odense, and Finding Joy With the National Team

LARS'S FIRST day of work after joining OB is met with the challenge of finding a place to live. It is customary for the club to assist new players with practical matters, but for some unknown reason they haven't been able to find an apartment for the new striker.

Shortly after his arrival at the office, OB's right-back Lasse Skov enters the room. He immediately recognises the new acquisition. Lars and Lasse have had several duels against each other as youth players; Lars as a left-winger and Lasse as his direct opponent at right-back.

They nod in recognition, and Lars explains that he has come to the office because he doesn't have a place to stay. Lasse then offers him shelter in his two-room apartment. Lasse's generosity warms Lars's heart and makes him feel at home in his new club and city. He immediately accepts the offer.

'I now had a place to live, and Lasse's offer was something that warmed me from within. I thought, "Wow, what kindness!"' Lars recalls, reflecting on the experience that sets the tone for his stay in Odense.

Lasse's generosity is just one of many positive experiences for Lars at OB. Despite its status as a top Danish club, OB is characterised by warmth and camaraderie. There is something genuine and almost familial about the club and its people, which has a healing effect on the wounded soul of Lars.

'It was good for me to experience the warmth in OB at that time, from the leaders, coaches, and team-mates, especially because I came from the opposite in Holland,' Lars says.

In Odense, there is no Golf GTI available, but Lars doesn't need one. Instead, he buys an old bicycle for 100 kroner and uses it as his means of transportation to training in Ådalen. The route takes him from Lasse's apartment in the city centre, down along the Odense River. Lars remembers many happy sunny days in his new city.

'In some way, I fell in love with Odense. I felt comfortable, able to breathe again, started living, was present, relaxed, and enjoyed going to training and playing matches,' Lars says. He also starts going out, visiting cafes or nightclubs, where he meets girls and enjoys various experiences.

After about a month in Lasse's small apartment, Lars moves into a larger one on Vestergade, a pedestrian street, together with another OB player, Jan Lewandowski, and Dorthe Bordingaard, sister of team-mate Keld Bordingaard. The apartment has a much better view.

'I would sit up in the window and enjoy the summer sun and the sight of all the girls walking by on the street below,' Lars recalls. 'I was single and wanted to find a woman who could make me happy.'

And she is not far away. Charlotte works in the clothing store beneath the apartment, and one evening, Lewandowski invites Charlotte and her friend to the apartment, where Lars becomes fond of the sweet Søndersø girl. Lars and Charlotte fall in love over the late summer, and their relationship turns out to be long-lasting.

The late 1980s becomes a very happy time for Lars. However, as he reflects, it is also 'the only extended period I remember as being happy and harmonious'.

As room-mates, machine worker Lasse and Lars develop a strong friendship with many long conversations in the late evenings and nights. They share a passion for sailing and spend many hours at sea in Lasse's sailboat. Lasse is also a promising footballer. He has played in the national youth teams with Michael Laudrup and Jan Mølby and will become a Danish champion with OB and a cup winner with AGF during his career. But he is also an energetic and resourceful man with many interests and dreams outside of football – a person who manages to turn dreams into reality. Lasse has just returned to OB and top-level football after a sabbatical year that included sailing around the Mediterranean in his own boat. This happened when he was in his prime as a player.

Lasse's stories and beliefs trigger thoughts in Lars, who has also experienced the gut feeling of wanting to 'get away from it all' and break free from the familiar routines. To skip all the externally imposed expectations. But Lars has never considered following his intuition and satisfying his inner joy as a realistic possibility. He is a professional footballer, a dream for many, and he has the skills to succeed. He has worked hard to get where he is, made sacrifices, and never given up despite the scepticism during the transition to the 'big clubs' inside Freja, the complete loneliness upon arriving at Brøndby, and the two cursed years in the Netherlands. And right now, he is doing really well at OB. Football is a pleasure, even a pure delight.

As a team-mate, Lars also benefits from his close bond with Lasse. Through him, Lars quickly becomes an integral and social part of OB's squad, which, at that time, is characterised by a relatively flat hierarchy and a good atmosphere across the first and second teams. At OB, the hierarchy is topped by standard-bearers like midfielder Ulrik Moseby and goalkeeper Lars Høgh. However, they assert their authority in an inclusive and friendly manner, which is far from the authoritarian cynicism displayed by Joop Hiele and Sjaak Troost at Feyenoord.

At OB, there is no need for excessive physical dominance or putting newcomers in their place, as was the case at Feyenoord. Even though they are competitors, they can still be friends on OB's top team.

'There was a special atmosphere in the team. Openness, helpfulness, hospitality, and lack of seriousness made me feel comfortable and immediately part of the entire team and squad,' Lars describes. Despite being competitors, Lars looks up to Moseby and Høgh and is fine with their roles in the squad.

'Lars Høgh was a focal point and a good friend. The diplomatic guy you could talk to, and he would crack a joke to lighten the mood. And then there was Ulrik Moseby. For an Intertoto Cup match, he might show up in his painter's clothes if he had just been painting his fence. That would have been unheard of in Holland, and you would have been fined if you arrived dressed like that.

'But it wasn't a big deal in OB. It was just what he did. And in my eyes, it was great to have someone who behaved naturally and took responsibility for his own life. He should be able to paint his fence and then give 100 per cent in a match. He was a hard worker who gave everything he had.

'And that's how we all did it in the OB squad.'

Lars also develops friendships off the field. He goes on sailing trips with Lasse, attends wine tastings with Ulrik, and is part of a four-man group that plays the card game whist on the team bus. He often finds himself by the pool table and, in general, experiences different and more positive relationships with his team-mates than in the Netherlands.

A budding friendship also arises with strike partner Per Pederson, six years younger than Lars. The talented striker, who will later have a career with the national team and abroad, including a spell at Blackburn Rovers, suffers a serious injury in Lars's debut match. He tears his cruciate ligaments in a collision with Brøndby's goalkeeper Peter Schmeichel. This means a six-month break for the young star, who had impressed with seven goals in the spring matches.

Although they don't play much together during this period, a good chemistry quickly develops between the two, and they spend many hours together. Per is also hospitable when Lars needs a place to stay during the renovation of his own new apartment.

'Lars was a fantastic guy. Fun, genuine, friendly, and polite to everyone. He was generally popular in the club and in Odense,' Per recalls. Lars enjoys being well-liked and having people around him who provide the security he has long missed. But even in such safe surroundings and with people who care about him, he still doesn't open up about his innermost thoughts.

'We were great friends, but not on a deeper level. We were close, but not to the extent that we talked about family or personal problems. But it was a good friendship, and I was closer to Lars than many of my other football team-mates,' Per says.

Lars's regained wellbeing on and off the field immediately translates into a handful of goals. In his debut for OB against his former club at Brøndby Stadium, he beats Schmeichel once, and after his first three matches, he has scored five goals in the first division.

There are no towering expectations for Lars to become a goal king in Odense. A modest return of nine goals in two seasons at Feyenoord downplays any expectations. However, Lars quickly shows that his years in the tougher Dutch league were not wasted. He thinks and acts faster than in Randers and Brøndby, quickly becoming one of the biggest stars at OB and in the Danish first division.

'He was a fantastic striker, maybe the best OB has ever had! And due to his abilities, he achieved a high status in the club,' Per claims. He is supported by Lasse Skov, 'Lars was really talented. And when he joined OB, he was a level above the rest of us. But it was also clear that he enjoyed being back in a freer environment and that there were people who appreciated what he did on the field.'

The difficult years in the Netherlands have also made Lars more appreciative of the success he is experiencing in Odense. He is the team's new star, but his team-mates notice nothing but his humble attitude towards himself and his personal success. During the autumn season, Lars scores 14 goals in 16 matches.

'He was a calm and quiet person off the field, and his success never changed him,' Per notes, also highlighting Lars's moderation and financially prudent lifestyle: 'Lars was generous toward the people he cared about, and never held back from giving. But he was also someone who, despite being able to spend more, would prefer to go on a last-minute vacation. He wasn't stingy at all, but why pay for an expensive hotel in Ibiza when you can go on a last-minute trip?' His successful return to the top Danish league will soon grant Lars several trips to excellent hotels, free of charge.

The village boy's national team debut

On the last day of August in 1988, Denmark are scheduled to play an international match in Sweden. After the glorious mid-'80s era, the national team is undergoing a challenging but necessary transition. In 1988, Denmark are eliminated from the European Championship after three defeats, and national coach Sepp Piontek is now in the process of building a new team, primarily with the aim of qualifying for the 1990 World Cup in Italy. The friendly at the Råsunda Stadium in Stockholm is a welcome opportunity to prepare the team for the upcoming qualifying matches, test new players, and explore tactical options.

To orchestrate the creative play, Piontek still has Michael Laudrup, 24 years old yet experienced, and his brother Brian – five years younger – who will primarily operate on the wings. However, Piontek lacks a dedicated striker, a goalscorer.

The legendary Preben Elkjær has not officially retired. He has returned to Denmark and Vejle Boldklub, is still only 30 years old, and in principle, available to Piontek. However, increasing injuries and a lack of form prevent Elkjær from truly regaining his old levels. Instead, Piontek selects 22-year-old FC Köln player Flemming Povlsen and the slightly older Lars Elstrup, both of whom were named Discovery of the Year in 1985, with Povlsen receiving the honour as a first division player. Now, they have both gained international experience, for better or worse, but for Lars, the red national team jersey is an entirely new experience.

At youth level, Lars has never come close to being selected for any of the Danish Football Association's national teams. However, his impressive performances and goalscoring form at the start of OB's season have impressed Piontek.

Lars receives the call-up with joy but also with a lot of uncertainty. It brings back memories of when he first stepped into the locker room at Randers Freja after his move from IF Fjorden. Doubts nagged at him back then too: was he good enough? Could he meet the higher level? Could he hold his own among the 'big' players? Now, he is selected for the senior national team.

Once again, doubts and uncertainties arise in his mind. How will he thrive among the big names? Among the 'stars'? Is he good enough? Does he fit into the team?

Therefore, feelings of inferiority become an unavoidable part of Lars's baggage on his journey from Funen to his first national team gathering in Vedbæk, a couple of days before the match against Sweden. However, he is otherwise in a good way, and it reassures him that he has familiar support on the trip.

'I felt really good at OB. Additionally, our masseur at OB, Allan Poulsen, was also the masseur for the national team. He was a focal point with his humour and good spirits,' says Lars. 'In that way, it was nice to have a friend by my side, and it made me feel comfortable, even among the stars on the national team.'

And, importantly, the meeting with Piontek turns out to be a positive acquaintance.

'Piontek was a really lovely person with a good sense of humour, and I really liked him. Maybe the training methods were a bit old-fashioned, but he was nice to be around. And he gave me the freedom on the field that I needed,' adds Lars, who is positioned as a second striker just behind Flemming Povlsen against Sweden.

It is an exciting combination because Povlsen is a strong and team-oriented forward who may not necessarily score the goals but creates space and opportunities for his team-mates, especially those with a nose for goal.

'Goalstrup' in focus

Back home in Råby, the Elstrup family sits eagerly following Lars's debut. Father and former football official Tage's heart beats with joy and pride as Denmark's national anthem, 'Der er et yndigt land', plays, and the camera pans across his son's face. The pride of the local shopkeeper reaches new heights as Lars connects with a pass from Brøndby player Kim Vilfort and scores to make it 1-0. Tage becomes so excited that he pounds his strong fists on the coffee table, leaving a visible reminder of his son's successful national team debut.

When Lars scores his second goal, Tage's reaction is a more subdued outburst of happiness. In that moment, he reflects on his son, who was once small and cautious, often standing unengaged on the sidelines during youth matches for IF Fjorden. Now, he sees the same son breaking free from the physically strong Swedish defender Peter Larsson and subsequently smashing the ball into the corner behind the legendary goalkeeper Thomas Ravelli. Emotions overwhelm the otherwise tough man, and tears run down his cheeks.

Lars's two debut goals secure a 2-1 victory over Sweden, giving Denmark their first win at the Råsunda Stadium since 1937.

The next day, the newspapers are full of praise for the 'village lad who outshone the Swedes', and *Ekstra Bladet* gives Lars the nickname 'Goalstrup' as a not-so-subtle reference to Preben Elkjær's nickname 'Målkjær' (Goalchaser).

'The two years in Holland taught me how to use my body, not only in the Dutch league but also in European Cup matches, and it paid off in my debut for the national team,' explains Lars to the same newspaper, without letting his feet leave the ground. 'But I don't want to take all the credit. Both Vilfort and Bartram's deliveries were excellent. Overall, everyone fought with such intensity, and I was carried through my debut in a splendid manner. I was fortunate to be in the right place at the right time; next time, it might be someone else who scores.'

Lars's two goals immediately generate interest abroad. Among those in attendance at the game is FC Köln coach Christoph Daum, who had previously brought Flemming Povlsen to the club. However, when confronted by the press with the rumours, Lars reveals that his time in the Netherlands has made him wiser and clarified his personal priorities. 'I am happy here in Odense, and it would take a very attractive offer for me to leave. It's not just about money. There are other things in life besides finances. It also needs to be a place where it's pleasant to be,' Lars tells *BT* on 9 September 1988.

And he means it. He doesn't want to experience what he went through in the Netherlands ever again. He is content in Odense, enjoys playing football for OB, and loves his girlfriend, Charlotte. Those are the essential factors for Lars right now.

Eight goals in 12 national team matches

Following his explosive debut, Lars is guaranteed a call-up to the national squad for a couple of crucial World Cup qualification matches in the autumn. He is brought on 12 minutes before the end of the away match against Greece, but two weeks later he starts in Copenhagen's Idrætspark against Bulgaria.

Before the match, Lars is brimming with confidence, boldly stating to the quote-hungry sports press, 'Give me the chance, and I'll score!' The remark underlines his transformation since returning from Feyenoord. He believes in himself again, both as a player and as a person. He knows he can score goals and feels he can live up to the expectations placed upon him by himself and those around him.

After nine minutes he confidently strikes the ball past Bulgarian goalkeeper Iliya Valov, but the visitors equalise, resulting in a disappointing 1-1 draw and marking an unsatisfactory start to the World Cup campaign for Denmark.

But Lars is riding a wave and scores again as Denmark leave behind the encroaching winter chill to win a friendly 2-0 in Malta.

In the first match of the spring season, Lars starts with a goal and plays a significant role as OB face the defending Danish champions, Brøndby.

He also finds the net in a friendly against Canada in April, but the spring season in the first division concludes on a sour note for Lars, who experiences a rare red card in June. To make matters worse, he is accused of violence. It is more than he is willing to bear, so when he is interviewed in *Ekstra Bladet* before the match against England in June 1989, he rages, 'I feel falsely accused of violence, and it puts a dampener on the excitement of starting in the national team match.'

The reason for Lars's anger is that a couple of weeks prior, he was shown a red card in a match against Frem. Lars and the Frem player exchanged kicks and were both sent off. Although OB win 2-1, the victory isn't what fills Lars's mind after the match. Referee Axel Larsen has reported him for serious violence, resulting in a lengthy suspension leading up to the England match.

'The harsh punishment not only hurts me, but it also makes me nervous about not being able to perform at my best,' Lars further states when asked about the incident. He is clearly irritated by the situation and feels unfairly treated. But his national team selection gives him an opportunity to get away from the turmoil and showcase himself positively at home in Idrætsparken, not only against England but also in the Danish Football Association's subsequent 100-year anniversary tournament, which includes participation from arch-rival Sweden and the mighty Brazil.

It is also Lars's chance to prove that he is the man to rely on in the crucial World Cup qualification matches against group leaders Romania in the autumn. Flemming Povlsen and Brian Laudrup have secured the two starting positions in the Danish attack after both scoring against Bulgaria in a 2-0 victory and each finding the net in the 7-1 thrashing of Greece. These wins have put Denmark back on track for the World Cup, but they have also pushed Lars further away from the starting line-up.

However, his competitive spirit has been ignited. And despite his potentially inhibiting suspension, he remains optimistic before the match against the English. 'Hopefully, I've managed to maintain my goal appetite. I've scored five times in nine national team matches, and I would be more than satisfied with just one goal against such a talented goalkeeper as Peter Shilton,' he tells *Ekstra Bladet*.

His wish is granted. After 56 minutes he receives the ball on the edge of the penalty area and, without hesitation, smashes it past Shilton with a powerful strike. The goal secures a 1-1 draw for Denmark and provides Lars with a renewed dose of confidence, which leads him to score twice in a 6-0 triumph over Sweden the following week. In the subsequent match four days later, Lars gets to enjoy the experience of playing the full 90 minutes. It happens in a vibrant 4-0 victory over Brazil on a scorching hot day in a packed Parken Stadium.

But Lars is definitely part of the national team's core group, in every sense. He may not be the one who takes up the most space or speaks the most, but he has earned his team-mates' respect with his play and gentle nature. And his goals: eight in 12 national team matches.

7

From Odense to Luton

SPORTINGLY, THINGS are going well at OB, but in the summer of 1989 the club is plagued by severe financial problems. When benefactor and main sponsor Kjeld Poulsen goes bankrupt with Bendix Bank, it means that the club can't afford to pay the players' wages.

Lawyer Jørn Bonnesen is busy cleaning up the troubled operation, and he knows that Lars Elstrup is the club's most valuable asset. In less than a year Lars has gone from a failed professional in another country to being the leading name at top-tier OB and a significant goalscorer for the Danish national team.

During the spring, buyers from West Germany's FC Köln and Italy's Fiorentina, among others, have shown interest in him, but in the end, only FC Nürnberg in the Bundesliga and England's Luton Town come forward with serious enquiries.

Bonnesen knows that Lars can provide much-needed money for OB. But it's also clear that Lars is content in Odense. He vividly remembers how his previous foreign adventure turned out. On the other hand, he also knows that this might be the move that can secure his financial future for the years to come. And it tempts the early matured savings bank customer and bank-educated player, who is fuelled by a new-found self-confidence, by Charlotte by his side in Odense, and by potential new adventures.

Lars has seen a new world open up before him. And he's ready for another one. On his own terms.

A tough negotiator

When Lars hears about Luton's interest, he quickly makes it clear to OB and Bonnesen that a move can only be considered if the financial benefits are evenly shared. In other words, Lars wants half of the transfer fee, which is an unheard-of demand. OB's management are not thrilled with the striker's stance but do not have much bargaining power. Lars knows that. He makes it clear that it's a 'take it or leave it' offer, and OB agree to his terms. First, Lars visits Nürnberg to attend a home game and hear what the Bavarian club has to offer. The Germans present their offer, but it's not attractive enough. Lars isn't in a hurry and declines. On the other hand, the small but quite successful English First Division club, Luton, is more proactive.

On a Saturday in late August, Lars travels to England to negotiate a contract with Luton. The plan is to sign it and then attend Luton's away game against Tottenham Hotspur in the afternoon.

However, Lars never gets to see that match – because he is a tough negotiator. He has allied himself with lawyer Kjeld Johnsen, a friend of the Elstrup family, and together they scrutinise Luton's offer several times. They reject some parts and ask Luton to make adjustments before finally reaching an agreement late on the Saturday evening after nearly 14 hours of negotiations.

Thus, it's a tired Lars who goes to sleep in his hotel room that night. He has secured a two-year contract with

Luton at a significantly higher monthly salary than at both Feyenoord and OB.

The total transfer fee of eight million Danish kroner (worth £850,000 at the time) remains for a long time the highest Luton have ever paid for a player. And it's for a man who may have grown up with English televised football but never saw himself as part of the Saturday entertainment at English stadiums.

'I had also sat and watched English football matches on *Tipslørdag* (Denmark's *Match of the Day* equivalent) and found them exciting. And England seemed like an exotic country to me, with the English language and driving on the left side of the road,' says Lars with a slight laugh.

'But when the offer came, I had no ambitions for a professional career, not even to come to English football.'

But now he's here. In England, with fresh ink on a new foreign contract. In his hotel room in Luton, Lars ponders how things can suddenly turn around. Unpopular and scorned at Feyenoord 14 months ago, now a highly valued acquisition in one of Europe's top leagues. Depressed and lacking self-confidence in the Netherlands, positive and assertive in Odense, and now in England.

But the next day, doubt creeps in.

Big expectations, bigger strength

Luton have high expectations for Lars, but his success at OB has strengthened him. It has given him more confidence. Just the day after signing the contract, he is out on the training field, eager to showcase his abilities.

In England, Lars is allowed to train harder than ever before, and for good reason. Physical training is more emphasised in English football compared to the Netherlands. Additionally,

Luton is a small club without big stars or technical players. It's not dribbling and technical finesse that will ensure the team avoid relegation, but rather hard work across the entire pitch. At Luton, physical training is not a form of punishment, but an inherent foundation in their collective self-perception.

From the start, Lars gives everything he has in the demanding and intense sessions. Intense interval training on the field may sometimes result in a trip to the sidelines to vomit. However, Lars doesn't give up. Again and again, he recalls his father's voice from childhood games. The voice that demanded Lars do better next time, fight a little harder, never give up.

Although this voice has in many ways hindered him and made him feel inadequate, it also pushes him, has toughened him and has taught him never to give up. And in situations like this, that's exactly what he needs. He won't capitulate, and he has no intention of showing the slightest weakness. He quickly earns the respect of his team-mates with his endurance and willingness to push himself to the limit. The British players know how to appreciate a foreign player who doesn't complain about the hard training but instead gives everything he has.

Luton's manager is Ray Harford, but the training is primarily led by his assistants, Jim Ryan and John Faulkner. Both of them gain the respect of the Danish player with their team management and football knowledge. Their training is varied and informative.

'In many ways, Ryan and Faulkner can be compared to Ernst Netuka. The two of them also gave me the freedom to play my game and were good at correcting small aspects of my play that could improve me,' says Lars.

The English league is already under way, and Luton have had a far-from-ideal start to the season. They are at the bottom of the table because they haven't been scoring enough goals. The hard-training Lars is now expected to help solve that problem.

Doubt creeps back in

Luton is located 30 miles north-west of London, with a population of 225,000. It's known for its airport, the Vauxhall Motors car factory, and its historic hat-making industry. It's a relatively anonymous and aesthetically unappealing provincial town, and Lars already has his first negative experience the day after signing the contract.

It's a grey and quiet Sunday morning when Lars leaves the hotel and takes a walk around Luton's town centre. Suddenly, he feels doubt creeping into his mind.

'As I walked down the pedestrian street in Luton and looked at all the sad and boring houses, I thought, "What on earth have I gotten myself into? Do I really have to be here for two years? I want to go home!"' he admits.

'So the day after signing the contract, I simply regretted it. And I distinctly remember calculating that there were 729 days left on the contract. But I was raised to live up to the expectations of others, so I saw no way out of the agreement.'

Lars moves with Charlotte into a larger townhouse in the Eddlesbury district outside of Luton.

Luton's stadium, Kenilworth Road, holds about 13,000 spectators, and it is surrounded by rows of houses in typical English fashion. It has been converted to an all-seater format and is notorious for its artificial turf, which was a subject of debate in the English football community in the late 1980s. The artificial grass actually resembles plastic more than grass, causing the ball to bounce differently and more forcefully than on a normal grass pitch.

However, the surface doesn't deter players, whether on the same team or opponents, from sliding into one tackle after another, and the abrasions are clearly visible after home games. Artificial turf is not something that scares Lars, as he has trained extensively on it during his time at Feyenoord. He can even see the footballing possibilities in the surface, believing it makes it easier to play his style of technical football.

All in all, the controversial artificial turf is seen as a minor detail for Lars. There are other, more significant challenges awaiting him.

Difficult start

For Tage, it is a big deal that his son is now going to play football in England. He has been following the English league on *Tipslørdag* since the programme started in 1969. Every Saturday afternoon during the season, Tage settles comfortably in front of the TV with his betting coupon and a beer by his side. Often, his sons also join him.

Tage is a fan of Manchester United, but he's perfectly fine with his son playing for Luton. And deep down, he is extremely proud that his son is playing in the prestigious English top division (which will be renamed the Premier League three years later). Lars himself is quick to invest in a satellite dish so that his father can keep up with the matches from England, which are now broadcast more frequently and on various satellite channels. Sometimes, even Luton and Lars are featured in the programmes.

'We have never asked anything of Lars, not even when he started earning a lot of money. He has always taken care of himself since he moved away from home,' says mother Ingelise.

'But when Lars went to England, Tage mentioned that he couldn't watch many of the matches from England without a satellite dish. So Lars immediately went out and bought a satellite dish for 1,200 kroner so Tage could watch English football.'

Lars makes his debut for his new club when he comes on as a substitute against Liverpool. The game ends 0-0, but the encounter with the English playing style requires adjustment for the Danish striker. In the first few matches, he barely touches the ball because it is constantly kicked over his head at a furious pace. And when the ball is at head height, Lars is never alone in challenging for it. In his first five matches he collides three times, forcefully, with an opposing player.

At that time, the English league is among the toughest in the world. In the late 1980s British players still make up the majority of player clientele, and this is evident in both playing style and refereeing decisions. Players almost have to be near death before a foul is called, and the game is played at a relentless pace that Lars finds hard to believe.

'I had a lot of freedom with responsibility as a forward, but I was still a bit surprised in the first matches,' he says.

'I liked to drop deep, receive the ball, play it on, and then move forward again. But every time I dropped deep, the ball was just hoofed over my head because it needed to go forward. It required some adjustment before I realised that I just had to stay up front and receive the ball there.'

In Lars's first ten matches, goals completely elude him, and the first critical voices begin to emerge against the club's most expensive acquisition. But in early October, Lars finally strikes. In two League Cup matches, Luton face Mansfield Town from the Third Division. In the first match at Mansfield's Field Mill, Lars finds the net twice in Luton's 4-3 victory, and in the return leg at home he further impresses with a hat-trick and an assist in Luton's 7-2 win. The first two goals are headers, and he completes his hat-trick with a cool left-footed finish.

The 'smaller' English cup holds great significance, and no clubs hold back their commitment or best players. Luton have even reached the League Cup Final in the previous two years, winning the first one. Therefore, in a couple of quite high-profile matches, Lars finally showcases his goalscoring instinct and flair for the English playing style.

Simultaneously, the five goals against Mansfield relieve the mounting pressure on him. Lars feels like he has contributed something and that he can score goals again, both for Luton and the national team.

'Last night went well in terms of scoring goals,' he says to *Ekstra Bladet* after the 7-2 match, adding confidently: 'I will continue today and tomorrow to show Sepp [Piontek] that I have never been more lethal. Since I came to Luton, I have become faster, physically stronger, and I have learned to go up in the air and head the ball into the net.'

He cheekily responds to the question of whether he should be the preferred choice in the upcoming crucial World Cup qualifying matches against Romania, 'Hopefully! My form is excellent, and my confidence is high.'

The local press is now full of praise, and even national journalists write about Luton's new 'goal-getter'. Brian Swain writes in his match report in the *Daily Mirror*, 'Elstrup was the best player.'

A 3-0 victory for Denmark

The goals against Mansfield conveniently coincide with the national team's crucial World Cup qualifying matches in the autumn of 1989. In his contract with Luton, Lars has carefully included a special clause that guarantees him time off for all national team matches he is called up for, including any friendlies.

Shortly after joining Luton, Lars is ready for the first two of such fixtures. 'I have a dream of making it to the World Cup finals next year, and that's why it's important for me to have time off for the match against Belgium on Wednesday and the match against Holland 14 days later, as well as hopefully many friendly matches leading up to the World Cup in the spring,' says Lars in *Jyllands Posten* on 22 August 1989, ahead of the two late-summer friendlies, in which he only gets playing time against Belgium, without scoring.

In the 2-2 draw against the Dutch, Sepp Piontek selects the Laudrup brothers and Flemming Povlsen for his offensive formation, and the same triumvirate starts in the qualifying match against Romania a month later. Lars has impressed and shown his goalscoring prowess in training, but unsurprisingly, he is left on the bench. Michael Laudrup's position is untouchable, and the dedicated and mobile Povlsen's spot is almost the same. And since his breakthrough in the 7-1 victory over Greece in May, Brian Laudrup has consistently shown great form for his German club Bayer Uerdingen, where he collaborates excellently with national team colleague Jan Bartram every weekend.

Lars's advantage lies, not least, in his ability to be a reliable goalscorer for the national team. But in Copenhagen's Idrætsparken Denmark will face a defensively strong Romania who will likely give very little away. Piontek therefore relies on Brian Laudrup's agile dribbling skills as the means to unlock the Romanian defence.

After 27 minutes, Brian Laudrup scores one of the best goals in recent national team history as he dribbles past three

Romanians and beats goalkeeper Silviu Lung. Defender Kent Nielsen opens the scoring after only four minutes, and Povlsen seals the deal five minutes before the end in a match where Brian Laudrup shines. There is no longer any doubt that it is him, and not Lars, who should start in the return match a month later in the Romanian capital, Bucharest.

A draw in that match and Denmark are ready for the World Cup.

A World Cup exit

It is 15 November 1989. A revolution is brewing in Romania, and a month and a half later, the long-time dictator Nicolae Ceaușescu is overthrown and executed during civil war-like conditions in Bucharest.

The new political upheaval affects the atmosphere surrounding the match. There is a mixture of eager anticipation, national pride, and a feeling of invincibility among the Romanians. This feeling is shared by the 28,000 spectators at Stadionul 23 August and deeply ingrained in the Romanian players on the field.

They are not shaken by Povlsen's goal after just six minutes or an early red card. They want to win. They want to make it to the World Cup finals.

From his place on the bench, Lars observes wave after wave of determined Romanian attacks rolling towards the Danish goal. Before half-time the Romanians have turned the Danish lead into a 2-1 deficit, and after an hour it is 3-1.

Lars's entrance on to the field 17 minutes before the end changes nothing.

The battle is lost, and it has been throughout the entire match.

'There was a special atmosphere in the stadium, and it was just one of those matches where I never had the feeling that we would win. Even when we were ahead and they had a player sent off, I always felt like we were the ones behind,' says Lars.

'They were the ones pushing forward, and they just kept attacking. We were constantly under pressure. There was never any respite, and we couldn't get a hold of the ball.

'When I was subbed on, I knew that I wouldn't get to touch the ball or be part of any teamwork. I would simply be overrun.

'And then you can always ask afterwards, how and why this and that. But on that day, there was simply nothing to be done.'

Romania win 3-1, and Denmark's World Cup exit becomes a reality.

Lars is disappointed. He is 26 and a half years old. A man in his prime footballing years, finding his momentum at a high European level. A wounded soul who has come back and rediscovered joy and dreams, and who dares to express and pursue them.

But the dream of the 1990 World Cup in Italy has vanished in the dark Romanian autumn evening. And there are nearly five years until the next World Cup finals in the USA. By then, Lars will be 31; will he still be active? And good enough?

In the meantime, there is the European Championship finals in 1992. But it's not something Lars thinks much about, even though it will be held just across the Oresund and Kattegat. The disappointment is too great right now. Denmark are out of the World Cup, and the highly regarded coach Piontek, loved by Lars and the other players, is about to say goodbye after 11 successful years.

National team dreams must be put on hold. And the focus must return to daily life at Luton Town.

Goals and pub visits

Back home in Luton, things are going well for Lars. He continues his success from the Mansfield matches by scoring in the subsequent league games. The first goal comes at the intimate and notorious Den in south-east London, where Luton secure a 1-1 draw against Millwall. The next goal comes in a 6-3 victory in Southampton, followed by another goal in a 3-2 defeat against Arsenal at Highbury.

Gradually, Luton start accumulating points, and before Christmas 1989 Lars is pleased that the team has moved away from the relegation zone.

Lars's positive trend is not solely due to his serious training efforts. He also feels comfortable off the field. The initial apprehensions he had when he first arrived in Luton prove to be unfounded. He receives a warm and friendly welcome from the locals. His relationship with neighbours, fans, and team-mates stands in stark contrast to his experience in the Netherlands. Even when the club is facing relegation, he receives nothing but positive encouragement when he meets fans on the streets of Luton.

'People warned me about hooligans when I came to England, but all the fans I met, both home and away, were friendly. Even when we lost, our fans would simply say, "Good luck!" or "Better luck next time!" So overall, I had only positive experiences with the fans and people in the town,' he says.

In many ways, Lars and Luton are a perfect match. The club has a down-to-earth atmosphere, and Elstrup's lack of goals at the beginning of the season is criticised more by the local press than by the fans. Many of the supporters are ordinary people employed at Vauxhall Motors and other factories in the town. They appreciate his work rate, fighting spirit, and humble approach to the game. They don't have exaggerated expectations for their local club, which is playing above its usual level by being in the country's top league for the fifth consecutive year.

Unlike his time at Feyenoord, Lars quickly finds his place in the social community with his team-mates. He has a special bond with goalkeeper Alec Chamberlain and midfielder Mark Pembridge, whom he often meets for a game of snooker. He also gets introduced to the unique English drinking culture. Although a Dane he enjoys the camaraderie and life in the pubs; he is not a big beer drinker himself and can only watch in amazement as his team-mates head to the bar. Mick Kennedy, in particular, stands out.

The tough-tackling midfielder has thighs so big that they often rub against each other and cause sores, yet he has an insatiable thirst for beer. Although Lars only plays with Mick in his first season, he manages to impress with his capacity for consuming hoppy beverages.

'One time after training, we went to the local pub to relax and have a drink. I was there for an hour and had one light beer. In the same amount of time, Mick managed to drink three or four pints of Guinness, and what was even more remarkable was that you couldn't tell at all!' Lars recalls with a chuckle.

Occasionally, Lars can't help but smile at his team-mates. But most importantly, he thrives in England's more relaxed approach to life outside of football.

'If a player in Odense was seen with a beer in his hand, it would be in the newspaper the next day, and they would be fined. It wasn't like that in England, where the culture was different. The attitude was that we controlled it ourselves as long as we were ready for matchday,' he explains.

Injured during the Christmas period

However, 1989 ends on a disappointing note as Lars sustains an injury during a home match against Nottingham Forest on Boxing Day. The injury requires surgery in his left knee, and will keep him out for up to six weeks. The injury does have a silver lining though, as it allows Lars to return home to Råby between Christmas and new year. Lars is well aware of his status in the small village of Råby and the place he has as a role model for many of the local children. Everyone knows who Lars Elstrup is, and everyone looks up to him. The fact that a boy from Råby is a top-tier English league and national team player is an incredibly significant thing in the small community.

When Lars is home, it becomes a major event, and in his typical proactive style, Tage is keen on arranging 'events' with his famous son. Lars willingly participates in various activities, whether it's signing autographs or being the target for shooting practice. His popularity only grows because he lacks any diva-like behaviour and enthusiastically contributes to creating memorable experiences for children and young people. For example, he allows a developmentally disabled young man to take multiple penalty shots until he successfully scores past him. He also distributes posters and autographs at his father's grocery store or at the local football club.

One particular episode is remembered by a local young boy. On the same street where the Elstrup family lives resides the Degn family. Their son, Christian, who is around nine years old and obsessed with football, admires Lars and aspires to be like him. It was a significant day for Christian when he received a letter from England during the Christmas season.

'I remember how big it was when Lars sent me a Christmas card from England. It made a huge impression on me that he would do something like that for a little boy he knew from the neighbourhood,' recalls Christian.

However, the boys from Råby can only have their hero in town for a few days after the turn of the year before Lars returns to England to patiently begin his rehabilitation.

French arrogance, Funen summer holiday

When Lars returns to the training field in February, it is with a new figure on the sidelines. Manager Ray Harford has been fired, and assistant Jim Ryan has taken over on a temporary contract. This change suits Lars. Harford is a more reserved manager, and Lars never develops a close relationship with him. It's different with Ryan, a former right-winger for Manchester United. Although his appearances in the red shirt were significantly limited by his direct competitor, George Best, there is still plenty to learn from the new Scottish manager and later the head of Manchester United's youth academy.

Lars finds Ryan to be very giving and inspiring, with training exercises that are always well-prepared and imaginative. But even though he trains with great enthusiasm and has a good relationship with Ryan, it doesn't change the fact that the Scot prefers big and strong Iain Dowie up front in the spring of 1990. The outspoken Northern Irish striker and future national team player joined Luton from the amateur club Hendon a year and a half earlier and is a classic target man. Currently, Ryan believes that Dowie is a more effective weapon in the air than Lars, who instead must watch Luton's desperate battle against relegation from the bench. It turns out to be a successful battle as Luton secure their survival in the top league with three consecutive victories over Arsenal, Crystal Palace, and Derby County, Dowie scoring crucial goals.

Lars also takes part in the season finale, but at the same time, it is clear that he has not been a major success in English football throughout the previous nine months. It becomes evident that Luton would like to offload their high-earning back-up striker during the summer break.

For a brief period, the club comes close to selling the Dane to the French club Brest, who include a young David Ginola (the future Tottenham Hotspur and Newcastle United star) in their team. Lars even travels to Brittany with Charlotte to get a closer look at the conditions at the French club and meet its officials. The parties are close to reaching an agreement, but during his stay in Brest, Lars encounters a version of French arrogance that spontaneously makes him back out of a potential contract.

'The club president in Brest kept me waiting, and the other officials just kept saying, "He'll be here soon … he's just about to arrive!" But in the end, I didn't want to wait for him any longer. So I got in my car and drove to Denmark for a summer vacation,' he says.

This sudden defiance turns out to be a good thing. Combined with new-found confidence and a special training session in Funen, this 'fuck you' attitude sets the stage for a completely different and more successful year for Lars at Luton Town.

8

The Reborn Goalscorer

THE SUMMER holiday back home in Funen is beneficial for both Lars and Charlotte. They are on familiar ground here. They can mingle with family and friends. They can enjoy the bright Danish days and summer nights. After the interrupted visit to Brest, they don't have to worry about any moving arrangements. Lars needs to complete his last year in Luton, where his wellbeing and enjoyment of the game usually outweigh the fear of not performing well.

But occasionally, dark thoughts overwhelm him. He feels that intrusive desire to 'get away from it all'. During these periods, he can't handle anything other than lying on the sofa when he's not training or playing matches.

Charlotte expresses her concern for Lars multiple times, as he can't explain why he suddenly feels this way. He has a good relationship with his team-mates and coaches in Luton. And he's content with his everyday life with Charlotte, who herself thrives in England. She understands the football world, yes, but she also has her own job, positive experiences, and encounters with new people. 'And we weren't lacking money or food on the table,' as Lars puts it.

Yet, these dark clouds appear, obscuring an otherwise sunny and seemingly privileged life as a professional footballer. They also overshadow the fundamental happiness of two young people in love with each other and life itself.

During these periods, the fact that Lars is financially secure doesn't help his financially conscious mind. Often, he visits his bank to get a bank statement. He sits down and looks at his substantial balance to see if it helps improve his mood. One of the reasons for switching to Luton was precisely the financial security. However, it's not a fact that provides healing during melancholic moments. He looks at the long string of digits, crumples up the bank statement, and throws it in the bin.

'Every time I felt depressed, I would pull out the bank statement, but unfortunately, it wasn't enough to dispel the depression,' he says dryly.

The money is good, but it also represents the entanglement and obligation that occasionally bother him and contribute to his melancholy. But in the summer of 1990, Lars experiences a form of rebirth within the familiar football setting.

Effective leisure training

Lars spends part of the summer maintaining his fitness at OB's facility in Ådalen. He meets up with his friend and like-minded individual, Per Pedersen, who, like Lars, has experienced significant ups and downs in recent years in football. Within a year, Per has been a top scorer, suffered a long-term injury, and become a Danish champion with OB (a few months after Lars's move to Luton). Now he's on his way back, and both he and Lars benefit greatly from combining social summer relaxation with a few hours of football training, including shooting, technical exercises, drills, and running.

'Per is a very pleasant person, and we stayed in touch throughout my time at Luton, always meeting up when I was in Odense,' says Lars, who clearly feels that the social ball game benefits him.

'I enjoyed myself, but I also got fit, and gradually, I started thinking, "Now I'm going to play my last year in Luton, so I'll give it my all!" So I thought, "Fuck it all!" because I felt like I had let go of something. Now, it was just about going full steam ahead and getting into top form.

'So I was well-prepared when I returned to England and had a fantastic second season in Luton.'

The summer training in Odense turns out to be a worthwhile investment because during the pre-season, Lars is allowed to train harder than ever before. But he isn't worried. On the contrary, he feels a mental shift occurring. He feels free, capable, hungry, motivated, inspired, and in top form. He feels, well, good enough.

Return to Scotland

In the meantime, Jim Ryan and assistant John Faulkner have taken over as the permanent management team at Luton. Under their leadership, the team embarks on a pre-season tour to Scotland. And Lars is ready.

This time, running, interval training, and occasional vomiting are supplemented with various team-building exercises in the Scottish Highlands. These innovative and different initiatives are well-received by the players, especially the newly motivated Lars.

'When I arrived at the training camp in Scotland, I felt a bit like when I arrived in Odense in the summer of 1988. I was happy and carefree. And then I just took one day at a time, giving it my all without thinking too much about things,' he says.

'The training was really enjoyable and different, and it made me feel comfortable. From a football perspective, it also allowed me to do things with the ball that I hadn't done before.'

Lars scores plenty of goals during the training camp in Scotland and impresses head coach Ryan, whose enthusiastic shouts of 'well done, Lars' echo across the Scottish fields as the Dane effortlessly hammers yet another ball into the top corner. Lars enjoys the training, and he appreciates the positive feedback from the coaches.

'I communicated well with Ray and John, and the two coaches also gave me some freedom, I thought. They instructed me so that I could do the right things for the team,' he says.

'Compared to before, the coaches, the training, and my own inner feeling were the significant differences. I clearly felt a positive trend, and it was just about going all out and experiencing this football year.'

When the season starts, Lars has secured a regular spot in the team. Not as a replacement for his competitor Iain Dowie but as the left sided forward in a 4-3-3 formation with Dowie as the centre-forward and his compatriot Kingsley Black on the right wing.

Lars quickly realises that when the ball is kicked long and high, which happens frequently, the archetypal British forward Dowie will likely win the ball in aerial duels. Therefore, it happens more than once that Lars manages to cut inside from the wing to receive the second ball from Dowie. This way, he avoids using his energy in duels with hefty defenders and can instead do what he does best: find space and utilise his finishing abilities. This is perfectly exemplified in the team's 2-2 away draw against Nottingham Forest on 1 December 1990, where Lars scores two of the most beautiful and illustrative goals of his career.

Goal magic at the City Ground

In the first sequence, the ball is kicked from Luton's half deep into Forest's territory, landing eight to ten metres from their penalty area. Lars finds himself between two Forest defenders. He starts his run just half a metre behind Des Walker, who is known as one of the league's fastest defenders. The other defender is already a couple of metres behind Lars with his initial sprint. Lars reaches the ball first and continues at full speed towards the goal, with Walker closely tracking him on his right side. On the edge of the penalty area, Lars shields Walker with his body and continues into the box with ruthless determination.

'There's not many people Des Walker can't catch, but Lars Elstrup is one of them,' observe the English TV commentator on the memorable race at the City Ground.

And indeed, Lars not only manages to maintain his speed with the ball against the lightning-fast Walker but also stays fully focused and dismisses the desperate sliding Forest defender in two moves before instinctively sending the ball through the gap between the onrushing goalkeeper Mark Crossley's legs.

It's a forward's goal that perfectly summarises Lars's key skills: timing, speed, physicality, awareness, and goal instinct.

In the second half, Lars scores one of the most dazzling goals of his career. It is a result of the choreography desired by the Luton coaching staff with the combination of Dowie and the Danish forward. On the edge of the penalty area, Dowie heads a precise long pass across to Lars, who is already in motion from the left side as the ball floats toward the Northern Irishman's accurate forehead. Lars, at high speed, nudges the ball forward with his thigh, allowing it to bounce once on the grass. In a split second, he can either continue his run into the box between the notorious England defender Stuart 'Psycho' Pearce and the sweeper behind him, or strike first time with his right foot.

Both scenarios are instinctively anticipated by Pearce and the sweeper, who act accordingly in a brilliant telepathic cooperation: Pearce quickly sliding down to block the shooting space while the sweeper positions himself as backup just behind. However, Lars does neither. He halts his run, as if flicking off a switch, narrowly evading Pearce's tackle while simultaneously softly nudging the ball backwards with his right foot. Pearce and the sweeper are now completely out of position, after which the once-restrained Råby boy turns his agile body diagonally backwards, swinging his left leg in a delightful strike on the ball. In an aesthetically curling flight, it sails into the top corner behind the goalkeeper, who had sensed the direction of the ball and thrown himself full length. But in vain.

The goal illustrates Lars's complete understanding of the team's playing concept, combined with the magic of intuition, agility, and kicking technique that, devoid of any national bias, rivals today's Messi or Ronaldo. Lars's top-level performance in December 1990 is simply of the highest international calibre.

At the same time, this scoring action also emphasises the fearlessness with which the defiant Lars approaches the challenges in the English top division. Pearce is a man who normally goes into tackles – on the ball or the man – with military precision. And he is a player that Lars and the other attackers in the league are notoriously afraid of. But Lars has been hardened during his time in England. He has survived encounters with an angry Vinnie Jones, who, as Lars diplomatically puts it, 'knew how to protect his territory'. And Lars has dodged for his life when a young and fiery Paul Gascoigne tried to take him completely out of the game.

And the goals keep crashing in from Elstrup's feet and forehead; for example, in a perfectly timed hat-trick at Carrow Road in the 3-1 victory over Norwich City.

These goals not only boost confidence but also earn points. In October 1990, Luton find themselves in seventh place, but Lars remains focused on the goal of survival. 'The squad consists of many good players, but we are very vulnerable if we suffer injuries. That's why it's good that we already have so many points,' he tells *Tipsbladet*.

It's a sober analysis because Luton will need those points towards the end of the season.

Back on the national team

While Elstrup primarily warms the bench for Luton in the spring of 1990, there is turmoil surrounding the Danish national side. Sepp Piontek has taken up a position as the Turkey coach, and a new German is brought in and presented with great media attention.

Shockingly, it turns out that the former Borussia Mönchengladbach player, Horst Wohlers, is not actually released from his coaching duties at Bayer Uerdingen. With red faces, the Danish Football Association has to admit that it has made a mistake. Instead, the association brings in Piontek's former assistant coach, Richard Møller Nielsen – also known as Ricardo – as his replacement.

It's a somewhat tumultuous situation just half a year before the start of the autumn's European Championship qualification campaign, but Ricardo knows the national team and its players. And Ricardo, from Funen, knows Lars from both the national team and his time at OB. And soon he will also know him as a sharp striker at Luton.

It has been a year since Lars was last in the team, but in the early autumn of 1990 Ricardo observes him several times. A week before Ricardo selects the squad for the first qualifying match against the Faroe Islands, he goes to Norwich to watch Lars pave his direct path back to the team.

Initially, Lars likes Ricardo, who previously had great success and led OB to the championship. But the switch from the popular and respected Piontek to the more humble and eccentric former assistant coach receives criticism from both the press and within the squad.

'Ricardo was a bit of an oddball, both in the way he conducted training and in the way he communicated with the press,' recalls Lars. 'You could get the impression that there might be a lack of respect around him. It wasn't something I thought about so much myself, but when others mentioned it, I could certainly agree with that viewpoint.'

Ricardo has difficulty handling the team's strong personalities like the Laudrup brothers, captain Lars Olsen, and especially Peter Schmeichel. And for Lars Elstrup, who needs security, it's not ideal that Schmeichel now has even more say.

Sometimes, the somewhat vague hierarchy leads to farcical preludes to international matches. Especially when the team's strongest players don't hold back from telling the press which tactics should be played. Under Piontek, there has never been any doubt about the distribution of roles and who is in charge, but with Ricardo, the power balance is much more uncertain. His tactical approach can be confusing at times, and many of the players simply struggle to relate to Ricardo now being the absolute authority.

Elstrup versus Schmeichel

Lars has a particularly difficult time with Schmeichel. It's not surprising, really. The Brøndby goalkeeper is Elstrup's polar opposite. While Lars is quiet and often self-effacing in his demeanour, Schmeichel is a man with towering self-confidence, bordering on arrogance. At the same time, the goalkeeper exudes a determination to win at all costs, which means his tolerance for mistakes from his team-mates is minimal. For Lars, this demand for 'perfection' strikes deep and is hurtful. Throughout his football career, Lars has struggled with perfection as a demanding ideal rather than a motivating one. And what Schmeichel represents to an extreme is exactly what Lars often wants to let go of: the incessant pursuit of perfection and the resulting outbursts of anger and denials when it doesn't work out.

Lars has seen how especially the defenders have received Schmeichel's thunderous tirades. And he doesn't like playing on the same team as the goalkeeper.

'At that time, I didn't like him,' he admits. 'I thought he behaved like an idiot when the ball went into the goal. It was directly uncomfortable to have a man like that on your team, and it made it really difficult to perform.'

But it's not only during matches that team-mates feel Schmeichel's temper. During warm-ups, he is notoriously known for verbally abusing the substitutes who are warming him up if the balls aren't placed exactly as he wants them or if they dare to score against him.

But one day, Lars has had enough of Schmeichel's outbursts and categorically refuses to warm him up. And during a simple training exercise before the home match against the Faroe Islands, he even dares to challenge the goalkeeper.

As part of the training, a four-against-two game is played, where the four players keep the ball away from the two in the middle who are trying to win it back, and then the player who loses the ball switches places with the player who wins it back. Whether it's the goalkeeper's poor technique or a deliberate act is unknown, but during these four-against-two games, it often happens that Schmeichel's passes are not going where they should be.

'He could intentionally send a hard ball to the team-mate so that it wouldn't be his fault if the ball was lost. Then he would just say, "In the middle," and he would stay out himself,' Lars recounts.

The same happens when Lars receives one of the goalkeeper's poor passes. When the goalkeeper's hard, hopeless ball is caught by one of the ball-hunting players, Schmeichel briefly looks at Lars and with a sense of entitlement in his voice says, 'In the middle!' But now Lars has had enough. In Schmeichel, he sees the embodiment of the authority he has silently submitted to for so many years, one he couldn't stand up against. He can't change his childhood, he can't go back to the training field in Dalbyovre and answer back to his father. But he can make a choice now and confront the authority when he encounters it. And it has to be over. He gathers all his inner strength, looks Schmeichel directly in the eyes, and challengingly replies to the towering goalkeeper, 'No, that was your ball!'

Inside, Lars trembles, but outwardly he remains cool.

'That day, I stood my ground, and a power struggle arose,' he recalls. 'He didn't give in, and neither did I. It was shocking for me to stand firm against the established goalkeeper. And for him, it would be a defeat if he had to go to the middle now.'

Seconds pass. The other players don't say much, they just silently observe the incident while Lars maintains eye contact with the authoritarian Schmeichel. After a minute, Michael Laudrup steps in and, with his usual diplomatic sense, he says, 'I'll take it,' and walks into the middle as the player trying to win the ball.

It's an action that adds weight to Lars's already positive view of the team's almost mythical star.

'He was a man who could talk to everyone. He didn't look down on anyone and helped create a good atmosphere. He had a very relaxed approach to being a professional. I really liked him,' Lars says about Michael.

But fundamentally, the aforementioned episode means that Lars shows Schmeichel that even though he is the quiet one, he won't just tolerate anything.

Goalscorer and benchwarmer

The European Championship qualifier against the Faroe Islands is the first significant international match since Ricardo took charge. And the coach desperately needs Lars's new-found goalscoring ability. In the first five matches without Lars under Ricardo, the team has only managed to score four goals, and the performances have been poor; defensive and without a trace of the champagne football they entertained the world with in Mexico four years earlier.

Therefore, it may seem somewhat absurd that several players tell various media outlets before the match that they expect to send the Faroe Islanders home with a 5-0 or 6-0 defeat. But perhaps they are indirectly referring to the fact that the Faroe Islands lost a friendly 6-0 against Brøndby earlier in the year.

Lars himself refrains from such bombastic predictions. But his confidence is high after his good start to the season with Luton, and Lars has a good feeling before the match against the Faroese, whom they defeat 4-1 with Elstrup scoring the second Danish goal.

The victory doesn't bring tranquillity to the team, and before the subsequent group match against Northern Ireland in Belfast,

Brian Laudrup is already designating himself and Flemming Povlsen as the attacking duo against their hosts.

'It would be the most correct to rely on us. We have previously shown that we can be successful. That's how we have to play tonight if we want to win. Of course, the national coach decides, but we are allowed to have our opinion,' Brian says to *Ekstra Bladet* on 17 September 1990, while his brother Michael is busy calling for peace and quiet among the players.

Lars doesn't need to speak in headlines or give the national coach advice through the press. He is also familiar with the British style of play, yet he starts the game on the bench.

Whether it's ultimately because the national coach succumbs to pressure or simply believes that Laudrup and Povlsen is the best combination up top against the Northern Irish is unknown. But it proves to be a poor decision. Povlsen doesn't produce anything and Brian Laudrup also doesn't achieve the success his big words in the press had suggested. Twenty minutes before the end, he is replaced by Lars, who, however, fails to make an impact on the game. The match ends with the same score as when Lars stepped on to the field, 1-1.

Denmark have already dropped an important point compared to their expected main rivals, Yugoslavia, who have collected full points in Belfast and at home to Austria. Besides being unsatisfactory in terms of results, the Danish play is poor and disjointed. And when Ricardo subsequently tries to bring things together in the dressing room, the atmosphere is icy.

Goodbye to Laudrup, goodbye to the European Championship?

The atmosphere is not much warmer – within the team or in the November air in Copenhagen – when a month later the team receives the group leaders Yugoslavia. Tactically and technically, the skilful Yugoslavians teach the crisis-ridden Danes a lesson in what appears to be an early and decisive result in the group.

Lars once again has to take a seat on the bench, from where he can see a point-thirsty but idea-less Danish team create absolutely nothing in the first 45 minutes. From the sidelines, the eager Elstrup is frustrated by the lack of offensive power, but he senses a glimmer of hope when Ricardo decides to take Povlsen off at half-time.

However, it is a surprise that Ricardo, instead of introducing Lars, calls midfield engine John 'Faxe' Jensen to his side. Journalist Carl-Johan Albrechtsen also wonders about this in *Ekstra Bladet* the day after the match: 'When it might have looked like a decent result at half-time, the national coach substituted striker Povlsen with the workhorse "Faxe". Not because Povlsen had been worth much, but then why not bet on Elstrup?'

Lars enters the field with 18 minutes remaining to replace Jan Mølby, but only to see Mehmed Baždarević hammer the ball into the net for a 1-0 Yugoslavia lead. Lars barely touches the ball in the next 15 minutes, and when Robert Jarni puts the Yugoslavians ahead 2-0, the match is decided.

If the atmosphere after the match against Northern Ireland was icy, it is tomb-like after this one. A few days later, the Laudrup brothers bid farewell to the Danish national team. They no longer want to play for Nielsen. There is speculation whether this is the beginning of a player revolt against Ricardo, but if so, it doesn't materialise.

The path to a starting position now becomes slightly easier for Lars, but it is in a national team without its most creative players and without the joy of play that he so desperately needs. And most likely, without a place in the 1992 European Championship finals in Sweden. First place is now far out of reach, and second place offers nothing.

'Staying up'

There is, on the other hand, plenty of joy in England, where Lars continues to impress. The week after the disappointment at Idrætsparken, he scores his eighth goal of the season in a 2-0 victory over Aston Villa. But the team encounters a series of injuries that slowly but surely push them towards the bottom of the table. Overall, Lars continues his good performance and his consistent goalscoring, but on the final day, Luton face another crucial game against Derby County, where the requirement once again is a victory to secure their place in the top division.

Kenilworth Road is filled to the brim with 13,000 excited fans. They finally find relief for their enthusiasm in the second half when Lars calmly rises in front of Derby goalkeeper Peter Shilton and decides the match and Luton's fate. The goal to make it 2-0 is also his 15th league goal of the season (with a total of 18 in all competitions), placing him ahead of competent goalscorers like Tottenham's Gary Lineker, Arsenal's Ian Wright, and Liverpool's Ian Rush. Lars has scored more than a third of Luton's goals and is hailed as a folk hero by the fans, who pour on to the artificial turf in their thousands after the final whistle.

On the scoreboard behind one of the goals, the blessed message 'staying up' blinks, and on that Saturday, no Lutonians go to bed early. But 'staying up' turns out to be a highly momentary truth. Despite the great success on the field and the team's rescue led by Lars, he cannot stay at Luton for much longer than the season-ending party that evening. The following year, Luton are relegated from the top division, while Lars has to struggle with his own relegation woes at Odense Boldklub, and to stay mentally afloat.

Staying up?

Gut feeling

After the survival party in Luton that May day in 1991, Lars and Charlotte are preparing to move back home to Odense. However, his goals and prominent performances have been noticed elsewhere in the English First Division, primarily by manager Howard Wilkinson at Leeds United.

'Howard Wilkinson contacted me and said he was interested in getting me to Leeds,' says Lars.

'I still had that belief that I should return to Odense. But I wanted to talk to him, so we met in Derby where we had a serious talk.'

Here, Wilkinson tells him that he is willing to offer a contract to the Dane. A considerable transfer sum and significantly higher salary would be a natural reality if Lars moved to Leeds, but Wilkinson has more temptations for Elstrup. Essentially, Wilkinson represents a traditional big club with a large and loyal fan base at Elland Road. Leeds have won several national and European titles, and in the recently completed season in the First Division they finished fourth. Wilkinson has even higher goals for the upcoming season and a sizeable player budget to pursue them with.

On top of that, Leeds are Lars's favourite English club from his days as a child, when he watched the weekly TV shows, and Wilkinson promises him that he and the team can fulfil the Dane's playing potential.

'As Wilkinson pointed out at the meeting, all the forwards he had signed became top scorers in the following season,' says Lars.

'And none of the forwards he had scored under 20 goals. And I would also come to that if I moved to Leeds, he said.'

That was most recently exemplified in Lee Chapman, whom Wilkinson fetched from Nottingham Forest just before 1990/91 and who scored 28 league and cup goals.

These are definitely promising words and exciting prospects that Lars is presented with, and which he takes with him on summer vacation in Funen. Despite all previous plans and feelings, he promises Wilkinson he will consider the offer.

But on his summer vacation, Lars also has an unresolved relationship with Luton Town.

Luton are pushing

1990 is five years before the so-called Bosman ruling is issued in Luxembourg, which allows professional European players to switch clubs for free after their contract expires.

Luton have absolutely no intention of just letting go of their Danish superstar, who has been the main reason for their continued existence in the top league. If the club wants, it can force the player to stay, as long as he receives a similar or better offer than the expired contract. However, the player can freely switch to an amateur contract at another club if he wishes.

The same goes for Lars, who jokingly says 'I hope they have forgotten it' when he has not yet received a new offer from the club in the late spring.

But the offer from Luton comes before the summer holiday, which puts Lars in a difficult situation in what should have been a relaxing summer break after a long, hard season.

He has long had a clear idea of returning to OB and playing there on a two-year contract. His last one. This is where he wants to end his career.

'I couldn't just say goodbye to everything while I was in Luton, so I had to end my career in Odense,' he explains.

'Even in the last year in Luton, where things were going well on the football field, there was something behind that did not match. And then I knew that I had to return to Denmark after my last period in Luton.

'At the same time, I knew that the two years in Odense would be my last, because I couldn't take it any more, didn't want to any more.'

But back home in Funen, Lars still had a major dilemma, because the decision was not quite so simple after all. The money-conscious banker within him also had some thoughts. All things considered, the money was not insignificant at Luton, and especially not at Leeds. The football-loving kid that he was, maybe he could be tempted by a season in a Leeds shirt? And then there was also the competitor who wanted to win matches and trophies.

He might be able to do that in OB as well, but in his current situation only as an amateur. And is his intuition really the right one to follow? What should he choose? What on earth should he do?

A stomach ache

Arriving in Næsby on Funen, Lars lies in the guest bed at his in-laws' place and relaxes. Or rather, he tries to, because inside his head, the favourable Leeds offer gallops like a wild horse.

'I lay there, about to make a decision whether to sign a contract with Leeds or stay in Denmark. But then I got such a stomach ache, it was absolutely eerie,' he recounts.

'And then I definitely knew I shouldn't go back to England. I shouldn't make that mistake again and go through another difficult stay. And I shouldn't deviate from the original plan, which was an inner and deeper desire for something else.

'Afterwards, I called Howard Wilkinson and told him that I wouldn't sign a contract with him or Leeds. I simply couldn't do it.' It is far from impossible that Elstrup actually declines an English championship on that summer day in 1991. Wilkinson, in any case, guides Leeds to become English champions the following season, with Chapman and new acquisition Gary Speed as the main goalscorers, while a certain Eric Cantona is brought to the team in February 1992.

It's a funny fact that today makes Lars smile more than anything else.

'Yes, that's the funny part of it all, it's crazy,' he laughs, and adds somewhat sheepishly, 'And it's also amusing to think that Wilkinson apparently saw me as one of the best players in the English First Division.'

But that has no significance for Lars in Næsby on that summer day when he feels so filled with anxiety that he can't imagine continuing with either Leeds or Luton under any circumstances.

He ultimately has to threaten Luton that he will return home and play as an amateur for OB if they don't make a transitional agreement with the Funen club, which would mean Luton couldn't demand any money for him at all.

This makes Luton show some understanding, and he is ultimately sold to OB for £250,000.

Comeback and personal success

Two months after playing his last match for Luton, Lars makes a comeback in Danish football. It happens on a sunny July day at Odense Stadium in the first Superliga match of the season against the working-class Copenhagen club BK Frem.

Although he has kept up with training, the tug-of-war between OB and Luton means Lars hasn't participated in many of OB's pre-season games. But the lack of match fitness is in no way noticeable when he showcases himself to the Odense audience. It's clear how his two seasons in the English First Division have made him even better than when he last appeared in the blue and white stripes. He is strong as an ox and constantly challenges Frem's Norwegian beacon Dan Eggen in one duel after another.

Lars naturally hopes to rediscover some of the joy he experienced during his first stint in Odense. And there is joy at the Odense Stadium when Lars, after 14 minutes, puts OB in the lead after a pass from veteran Keld Bordingaard. But he quickly realises that his new team-mates don't possess the same international class as he does. Particularly in defence, in front of the experienced Lars Høgh, things are not looking good. Despite another Lars goal, the match ends in a humiliating 5-2 defeat. For Elstrup himself, the game is a success, and the press subsequently agrees that he will be a great asset to the club.

They are right. Lars scores goals on a regular basis, and two months later he is at the top of the scorers' list with nine goals in ten matches, which is more than half of OB's 17 goals scored. At the other end of the field, things aren't going as well for the team, and OB are at the bottom of the table.

Despite the goals, Lars's body has started to cause him problems again. The years in England have not only made him stronger and better; they have also worn down his body. It's especially his ankles that give him trouble, and perhaps Lars's legs haven't fared well with all the matches on the artificial turf at Luton.

At the end of September, he and Charlotte move into a large 174-square-metre apartment in central Odense, which was previously inhabited by the former director of the bankrupt main sponsor, Bendix Bank. Charlotte finds a job as an assistant in a kindergarten in the backyard of the property, and they both enjoy having family and friends close by again.

Lars's performances on the field often contrast with his mood, which still swings into melancholy and despondency. He still enjoys playing football for OB and is recognised by team-mates and fans. But inside, the fear of not measuring up still lingers. There are days when he can't muster the strength to get up, can't muster the will to go to training, can't muster the energy to meet his team-mates, can't handle the pressure to perform.

However, he manages to stay afloat and has no problems finding his level in the actual matches, despite the injuries and mental struggles. However, they don't become less frequent or milder in severity during Lars's final two seasons in Odense. If anything, quite the opposite.

Red and white goal drought

Throughout most of 1991, Lars is out of the national team. His injuries are a significant reason, but when he gets the chance to represent Denmark he doesn't perform. He is appointed by Ricardo as one of the five guaranteed starters in the year's first international friendly against Bulgaria. But he disappoints, fails to create a single opportunity, and is substituted in the second half.

Without Lars, the struggling Danes rise in the Euro 1992 qualification group with an away victory against Yugoslavia and a home win over Austria. Denmark have thus positioned themselves back in the race for the group's top spot and the ticket to the European Championship if they take maximum points from their remaining games, and Yugoslavia drop points in one of theirs.

It is highly unlikely, and despite the impressive 2-1 victory in Belgrade, criticism of Richard Møller Nielsen remains massive. Among some members of the press, there is almost a hope that Denmark lose so that they can get rid of the coach.

There are also mixed opinions among the players about Ricardo, and there is real unrest behind the scenes when Peter Schmeichel lashes out at the coach in his book *Den Bagerste* (The Last Line). In it, the goalkeeper criticises the coach for focusing too much on hard work and not enough on forward-moving football.

Whether Lars's current international goal drought is connected to a more defensive focus is uncertain. But it is a fact that, in Nielsen's first two years, Elstrup scores a measly one goal in seven international matches and never resembles the player he was under Sepp Piontek.

Nevertheless, he is selected for the match against the Faroe Islands and included in the starting line-up. Denmark win 4-0, but the game becomes a major personal disappointment for Lars, as he gives one of his worst international displays. He never gets close to the ball and appears inhibited both physically and mentally. The atmosphere within the team could be better. Despite the improved results, there is still not much respect for Ricardo, and the lack of harmony is not beneficial for Lars. His poor performance against the Faroe Islands is followed by equally lacklustre displays in the qualification matches against Austria and Northern Ireland. However, Denmark manage to win those matches, but Yugoslavia don't stumble and secure the top spot and the European Championship ticket.

Denmark finish as runners-up in the qualification group, a position that is completely insignificant for over six months.

Setbacks with OB

Back in Odense, Lars doesn't have much to celebrate either. A disappointing autumn results in OB being relegated to the newly established qualification round of the Superliga, where they have to spend the spring fighting to return to the top division.

Despite the presence of capable players like the future assistant national coach Keld Bordingaard, a young Allan Nielsen, defender Steen Nedergaard, and Lars himself, there isn't much that works for OB. It's a very disappointing half-year for the club, which should have been a contender for trophies.

The sponsor Micro Matic has invested millions of kroner in OB, including bringing Lars back and paying his wages, which are significantly higher than the average. The goal was to compete at the top level, but for Lars, there awaits a stark contrast: matches against Nørresundby Boldklub, Vanløse, and Viborg less than a year after playing against Manchester United, Liverpool, and Arsenal.

Today, it's difficult for Elstrup to see what went wrong for OB in that half-year of the Superliga's regular season.

'We had a really good team with several players who had become champions just two years before and went on to achieve success again. But in that half-year, nothing worked. We simply couldn't win and ended up being relegated and playing qualification matches,' he says.

Although OB finish last, Lars's 12 goals make him the top scorer in the Superliga regular season. It's a small consolation when the club as a whole has disappointed. On the other hand, Lars is ready for the qualification round to guide OB back to the Superliga. That's what spring 1992 is all about for him.

9

Heading to the Euros

RUMOURS HAVE been swirling throughout the spring of 1992. If the civil war in Yugoslavia isn't stopped, the international community may intervene with sanctions against the regime in Belgrade. Yugoslav President Slobodan Milošević's government is not formally at war, but it supports the Serbian breakaway republics in Croatia and Bosnia. The sanctions primarily aim to hit Yugoslavia economically and commercially. However, they also lead to a boycott of sporting activities, which could result in the exclusion of the Yugoslav national football team, despite qualifying for the upcoming European Championship ahead of Denmark.

In mid-May, just one month before the start of the European Championship, nothing is yet settled. The Yugoslav squad even arrive in Sweden and begin preparing for the tournament. However, it is a completely different team from the one Denmark faced in the qualification group. Only the elegant midfielder Dejan Savićević remains from the original squad, and when confronted with the unfortunate situation his team and country are in, he simply states in *BT* on 4 May 1992, 'I am a football player, not a killer.'

Lars Elstrup, like the rest of the Danish squad, has been informed that Denmark may be called upon instead of Yugoslavia.

'We were advised by the coach that there was a small one per cent chance that we might still go to the European Championship if Yugoslavia was excluded. But within the team, we considered the chance microscopic and had already started looking forward to the summer vacation,' says Lars.

The major European leagues conclude in May, allowing the selected players to gather for the European Championship. However, Lars does not play in any major league. He plays in the qualification round for the Danish Superliga, which does not take into account the selected Euro players, so the final rounds of matches are scheduled just before the start of the finals on 10 June. OB are on track for a quick return to the Superliga, and Lars has already started looking forward to the holiday. He has also begun to enjoy the sunshine and the summer cottage while there is no training or matches.

However, in the other end of Europe, the early summer has a far from harmonious atmosphere. Reports from the troubled areas of Croatia and Bosnia depict murder and atrocities. On the last day of May, a series of published images of mutilated people from a queue in the Bosnian capital Sarajevo prompt a reaction from the United Nations. At a meeting in New York, the UN Security Council adopts Resolution 757, imposing a trade embargo on Serbia and Montenegro, including a requirement for UN member states to refrain from any sporting contact with the involved nations.

UEFA can only draw one conclusion from the UN resolution: Yugoslavia are immediately excluded from the European Championship, and their place is taken by the runner-up of their qualification group, Denmark. Their first match will be on 11 June against England in Malmö.

The Danish Football Association has a busy time making phone calls to the national team players who are scattered around various vacation spots in Europe. Lars himself is at his in-laws' summer house in Hasmark when the phone rings. He hasn't started his summer holiday yet but is sitting in the sun with a beer in his hand when he suddenly receives the message to prepare for the tournament.

'I was asked if I was ready to go to the European Championship, and of course, I answered "yes",' he says.

'We had been informed that there was a small chance we might go. And if the call came, we had to be ready, regardless of whether we were on vacation or whatever.'

Lars is in a good period both physically and mentally. He celebrates the news that he will soon join the European Championship squad by scoring the only goal in the home victory against Vejle the next day. The following week, he and OB secure promotion to the Superliga with a 5-1 victory over Viborg. While his team-mates party through the night, Lars heads to Sweden, where he is one of the last players to check in at the beautifully located team hotel in Ystad. There are just two days until the first match against England.

The atmosphere is initially quite relaxed, and the expectations for the team are non-existent. It is a psychologically perfect platform, especially for Lars. When asked by *Ekstra Bladet* how it feels to suddenly play in the Euros just before departing for Sweden, he replies, 'I don't feel tired. We are outsiders in the European Championship and happily free from performance anxiety in advance.'

While most players are happy for the opportunity, there are also sceptical faces. As striker Bent 'Turbo' Christensen says to *Ekstra Bladet* on 1 June, 'We simply aren't geared to be in it. It's incomprehensible that the decision wasn't made earlier.' On the other hand, Brian Laudrup, who has recently returned to the team, is more positive and believes that Denmark can only surprise.

However, within the squad, there is so much professional pride and such prominent winners like Peter Schmeichel, John 'Faxe' Jensen, and Kim Vilfort that the chance must be seized, no matter how slim it may be, but with a rational and balanced approach based on the actual realities.

'Many of the players had just been relaxing and on summer vacation, so there were no expectations, no pressure,' Lars says, summing up the atmosphere after his arrival in Ystad.

'It was like this, "Well, now we're in it after all, and that's good enough. Let's just take it from here and see how it goes." Now we give it our all, and if we lose, no one will be upset about it. We've done what we could.

'It would be a shame if we didn't win a match or advance from the group stage. But somehow, it was insignificant if we felt we had given 100 per cent.'

In principle, this is also the coach's attitude. The often criticised Richard Møller Nielsen turns out to be the right man to handle the sudden opportunity. He manages to balance the training sessions so that players who need it can sweat on the track, while those in need of rest can have that opportunity. This differentiation in training proves to be valuable later on. The tactical instructions are less confusing, and the coach knows what he wants and how to achieve it. However, initially, his tactical plans do not include Lars.

Firstly, half a year in the Danish second division has not increased his chances of a starting position. His late arrival at the camp hasn't helped either. And in terms of the counter-attacking style of play that the coach emphasises, Lars may not be the ideal type of player up front. In that regard, he is considered the third choice after Flemming Povlsen and Brian Laudrup, and faces increased competition from lightning-fast forwards like Torben Frank and Bent Christensen. The latter, currently playing for Schalke 04, has already proven his worth as the top scorer in Euro qualification, and Frank is the new rising star on the team. He has only played three international matches before the Euros, but he has just helped Lyngby become Danish champions and is soon to be named the country's Player of the Year for 1992.

However, Lars feels a tremendous momentum and senses the positive vibes within the squad. He wants to be part of it. He wants to contribute. He wants to play. He wants to score goals.

Goalless opener

On 11 June, 26,385 spectators fill Malmö Stadion for Denmark's opening match against England. The day before, Sweden and France had kicked off the tournament and Group A. Sweden have home advantage and a solid team built on the Swedish combination of down-to-earth common sense and unwavering confidence. All of this is enough to secure a decent opening result of 1-1 against a French team that is still in the early stages of building towards future world dominance. However, Sweden are certainly outsiders in the tournament.

Traditionally, England are also among the favourites, at least as believed by the English themselves. But Denmark have had good experiences against England, who field a couple of familiar defenders in Stuart Pearce and Des Walker from Nottingham Forest. Lars has a certain psychological advantage over them after his magnificent performance in Nottingham in December 1990, but he doesn't get the chance to start. Instead, Christensen is preferred as the centre-forward, but he doesn't get many opportunities in a disciplined and cautious affair that ends goalless.

It's a highly commendable start for Denmark in the Euros, but for Lars, it is very disappointing not to get any playing time. And he is not the only one feeling let down.

Tage Elstrup makes the trip to Malmö to watch his son, but he returns to Denmark without having seen Lars in anything other than training gear warming up and sitting on the bench.

'It was a dream for me to be able to watch him play in the European Championship. And when he didn't even get on against England, I was really angry and disappointed,' says Tage.

'Denmark had a couple of chances in the game where I thought Lars could have scored.'

Of course, the disappointment is particularly great for a knowledgeable father who wants to see his talented son in action. But Lars himself feels the internal flame burning through. He is in Sweden to play. He is just so ready.

Fortunately, there are only three days until the next match against their neighbours and arch-rivals at the Råsunda in Stockholm, the opponents and the arena where Lars made his national team debut with two goals.

'Denmark out of the Euros!'

As a general schedule during the Euro tournament, the days are structured as follows: wake up at 8am, followed by breakfast and training at 10.30am. Rest and relaxation take place between lunch and dinner. Quiet hours in the rooms are observed by 11pm.

Several times, the schedule is changed and expanded with alternative forms of recovery. The players visit a McDonald's restaurant, and one day they go out to play mini golf, while a planned fishing trip is cancelled due to the weather. Interestingly, it is the players at the top of the hierarchy who initiate these different forms of diversion. In this way, it is a constructive rebellion against the disciplined match preparation that many of them are used to at their clubs. The coach reacts positively and manages to strike a balance between the more serious preparation for the matches and the activities that help further bond the team together.

Outside the red and white universe, the informal Danish attitude raises some eyebrows, especially among the Swedes. In a Swedish newspaper, the Swedish coach Tommy Söderberg sends a sarcastic greeting to Lars, accusing him of just wanting to be home in Odense, drinking beer and having a good time. Additionally, a Swedish journalist nearly falls off his chair when Lars Olsen starts their interview with the obligatory cigarette.

For Elstrup, being in the team is only a positive experience. The atmosphere in the group is relaxed and down-to-earth, and it makes him feel really comfortable. The nagging pressure of expectation that often weighs him down seems to be eliminated to a large extent. And now, he just wants to play. To get 'into' the tournament.

However, he doesn't get that opportunity against the Swedes, who win 1-0. It is a defeat with prospects, though, for both Denmark and Lars.

Despite a desperate exclamation from TV2 commentator Jørn Mader that 'Denmark is out of the Euros' right after the final whistle from German referee Aron Schmidhuber, Denmark are not eliminated. On the contrary; Denmark holds their fate in their own hands.

Before the Sweden match, England and France played out a 0-0 draw. And as anyone with basic understanding, including the coach, could calculate before the showdown at Råsunda, a one-goal loss would mean the following: Denmark would still have a chance to advance with just a one-goal victory over France.

And perhaps that is precisely why Elstrup is not brought on in an all-or-nothing offensive after Tomas Brolin's goal in the 58th minute?

Self-assured benchwarmer

While Denmark made it to the Euros as a replacement, France won all their qualifying matches. Led by coach and legendary former player Michel Platini, they are also undefeated in 21 games. That streak needs to be broken if Denmark are to go further in this tournament, while the French can most likely advance with a third draw in the group. But they are clear favourites and will secure progress with a victory. They also play their role to the fullest, and arrogance fills the air as the two teams stand in the tunnel before the match. The Danes, meanwhile, motivate each other with shouts and encouragement, while a mocking silence is sensed from the French players.

Even though Denmark have to win, and they are still goalless after a total of three hours of Euro tournament football, Lars once again takes his place on the bench. After his disappointing performances, 'Turbo' has been dropped from the attack and replaced by Torben Frank.

Lars is disappointed. Irritated. Rejected. Extremely disappointed. But he is still in a good place mentally. And he speaks diplomatically when he comments on his apparently permanent role as a benchwarmer to *Ekstra Bladet*, 'As I have said all along, I accept the coach's decisions. But you can still be disappointed when you're not starting. If I complained, all nine players who are not in the team could do the same, and then it would be a disaster. I have been criticised by some pundits for not participating in the play from deep positions, and maybe I'm not as fast as the others. But my strength lies in front of goal. See the chances before the defence and exploit them. Simple as that. Just like I have done for OB for a long time.'

Looking back today, however, he is not as diplomatic. It is the competitive beast in Lars that roars the loudest.

'In the first two matches, I felt ready to start,' he says. 'I felt good in my legs and in my head. I felt that I was better than those who started and felt that I had something to contribute.'

But it is still a professional and focused team player who takes his place on the substitutes' bench at Malmö Stadion on 17 June.

A magical finish

After just seven minutes, the confident and strong midfielder Henrik Larsen – sometimes known as Store (translating as Great) – puts Denmark ahead. The majority of the stadium's 25,673 spectators are in ecstasy. Denmark's first goal in the Euros; right now, they are in the semi-finals.

The early lead also means that they need to defend well, guard their position, and avoid taking offensive risks. In such a game scenario, Lars's chances of getting on the field are minimal.

But it doesn't change anything. Lars is still sitting on the bench, deeply concentrated, and following the game. At the same time, he is completely within himself.

'I sat on the bench and was only focused on my own game. I've never cared about how the opponent looked, what their names were, or anything,' he says.

'So during the game, I was solely thinking about my own role and what I can do and am good at. And what I'm good at is playing the game simply, releasing the ball quickly, working hard, moving into position, making the right movements.'

Those virtues will soon come into play because France's Jean-Pierre Papin does what he did in the opening match against the Swedes and equalises after about an hour.

Throughout the game, the elegant left-back Kim Christofte has effectively marked the star striker, preventing him from getting significant chances. But the substitution of the advanced centre-back Laurent Blanc suddenly creates confusion in the Danish defence. Christofte is left alone with two opponents and loses Papin, who confidently shoots beyond Schmeichel.

Coach Nielsen must act quickly. He calls for Lars and asks him to warm up. Denmark and Lars have one mission in this game, and it's not rocket science. The team needs one thing: a goal.

In the 68th minute, Lars replaces Brian Laudrup. It may not seem like the most obvious substitution. Laudrup is the man who can open up the now increasingly compact French defence, but he is tired after a number of dribbles and challenges throughout the game. Right now, fresh energy and goal instinct are needed. Something that Ricardo believes he can find – not in Bent 'Turbo' Christensen on the bench or Laudrup on the field, but in Lars, who enters with full focus and an overwhelming sense of confidence.

'When I'm substituted on and step on to the field, I am happy and positive, knowing that I will get a chance to decide the game,' says Lars.

'From the first touch of the ball, I could feel that I was sharp. And I felt that we had the opportunity to win the game. It was just a matter of trying to take my chance and do something right, good, and constructive.'

All of Lars's accumulated energy and love for football now take centre stage in one of the most crucial sequences in

Danish football history. A game action that, in 11 to 12 seconds, transforms Euro '92 from a cosy story of a decent effort under difficult conditions that almost brought Denmark further in the group stage to the realised heavenly adventure that the Danish Euro campaign suddenly becomes.

Many Danish football fans still remember the goal itself: Lars, using the inside of his foot, taps in Povlsen's cross near the goal line. But the whole setup leading to the goal perfectly summarises what Lars has been focusing on while sitting on the bench, 'Playing the game simply, releasing the ball quickly, working hard, moving into position, making the right movements.'

We rewind the time, 78 minutes into the match. Lars has been on the field for barely ten minutes when he drops deep to receive the ball in the French half, near the edge of the centre circle. He has his back to almost the entire French team in an established defence. He controls the bouncing ball and elegantly shields it past a pressing French player, continuing into the centre circle with full ball control. He still has his back to the French goal.

For a few seconds, the five players closest to Lars are all French. Two of them are moderately pressing him from behind, while a third runs towards him from the opposite side of the midfield line. If Lars loses the ball here, a dangerous French counter-attack is imminent. But he doesn't. He remains calm and cautious, turning his gaze and direction towards Denmark's right side. For a brief second, he awaits right-back John Sivebæk's movement to a free position on the wing and delivers a simple, flat inside pass just before the threatening French attacker can intercept his pass to the flank. Sivebæk touches the ball for a first-time pass, and the ball floats in a balloon-like arc over two advanced defenders in what appears to be a failed offside trap.

The ball lands between the feet of Povlsen and Torben Frank, both of whom have moved towards the right side behind the defence. For a split second, it may seem like an offside, but no one reacts, neither the referee, linesman, nor players.

Just as the ball lands between the attackers' feet, Lars changes from a leisurely jog up the field to an explosive acceleration towards the penalty area. Povlsen misses his first touch, which momentarily looks like a wasted opportunity. But he quickly regains control of the ball and storms down the edge of the penalty area with a French player chasing him closely. Povlsen looks up and sends a hard, low pass past the two nearest defenders and into the path of the goal. The ball continues past Frank, who is positioned a metre too far back to take a shot. It slips past a third sliding defender and reaches Lars. Even before his rapid entry into the penalty area, he has spotted the marginally free space between the third and fourth defenders, and he accelerates purposefully towards the edge of the box. With instinctive composure, Lars lets the ball glide past his right foot and perfectly coordinates his left inside strike, sending the ball beyond the French goalkeeper, who has moved slightly out of his goal.

'LARS ELSTRUP! One is tempted to say, AGAIN!' shouts TV2 commentator Flemming Toft to the ecstatic football population in these seconds. Toft's voice almost cracks with spontaneous enthusiasm, and in front of the screen in Råby, Tage and Peter can hardly believe their eyes.

The goal is not so different from the many that Lars has scored before this one: a quick run into the box followed by a low shot. Many times throughout his childhood, youth, and adulthood, the youngest member of the family has scored in this manner. But the goal against the French is the most important he has ever scored and will ever score.

Seconds after scoring, he is overwhelmed by his jubilant team-mates behind the French goal. The stadium buzzes with a trembling jubilation, and Lars runs back on to the field, waving his arms towards the bright evening sky.

The French players stand frozen, and their desperate attempts to establish pressure in the remaining minutes are in vain. Denmark win 2-1 and advance to the semi-finals. Lars took the field and realised his inner focus. Pure magic.

10

The Unhappy Hero

The unfortunate hero of the European Championship

A substitution, 12 minutes of football, and a decisive inside pass. Lars Elstrup is suddenly the name on everyone's lips. Talked about, celebrated, praised. After the France match, the ecstatic press corps surround the goal hero, seeking his comments. But despite all the joy, he remains a calm and modest Jutlander, steadfast in his belief that football is a team sport.

'I repeat, the team is still the most important, and it was the team that stood behind the victory against France. If the defence hadn't covered well before the goal, and if Flemming's pass hadn't been so perfect, the goal would never have come,' Lars tells *Ekstra Bladet* after the match.

Twenty years later, the protagonist still maintains a humble approach to his own role in the historic group stage.

'I remember, of course, that I was happy because I scored, and it was an important goal,' he says. 'But for me, it has never been important or special that it was specifically me who scored. A football match is a team effort.'

Others can provide the lofty praise, and they do. Among them, Brian Laudrup, who calls Lars 'Denmark's Papin' in *Ekstra Bladet* says, 'I am full of admiration, simply put. Elstrup has a unique ability to strike when he gets the chance.' And with his usual knack for figurative language, Richard Møller Nielsen describes Lars as 'poisonous like insecticide'.

The goal not only brings him tremendous attention but also provides Lars with a sense of relief in relation to his own expectations. There is a significant difference between being part of the team when you have been in the game and when you haven't. And now Lars has not only gotten some minutes on the field but has also contributed constructively, even decisively.

'Now I felt like I had contributed something, and that allowed me to relax a bit,' Lars explains.

He is profiting from the team's relaxed yet football-loving attitude throughout the three initial matches.

'We simply took one day at a time, enjoyed playing, had fantastic camaraderie, and it got us to the last group match where we advanced,' he says. 'And then the feeling in the team was that "we can definitely win this".'

But there is still no burden of performance anxiety plaguing Lars, who is now part of a squad that is ready for the semi-finals and one of the players who has made his mark on the tournament. A player with expectations placed upon him.

And in the dressing room after the France match, Lars and the team simply did what they were already European champions in: enjoyed each other's company and lived in the moment in a relaxed unity.

'When you've won a match, made a physical effort and a mental performance, you celebrate a little,' he says. 'So we had a beer and a cigarette in the dressing room. We relaxed and enjoyed ourselves, talked about the situations in the game, and let the impressions sink in. And then we had the next match to look forward to four days ahead. But we didn't talk much about that yet because we didn't need to think too far ahead.'

On 22 June, the semi-final against the Netherlands awaits at Nya Ullevi in Gothenburg. Here, Lars returns to the bench but remains focused on himself and his game, with peace of mind.

Semi-final atmosphere

Leading up to the semi-final, the squad moves to the beautifully situated Stenungsund Yacht Club, 40km (25 miles) north of Gothenburg. From his hotel room, Lars and the other players can enjoy the view of the beautiful archipelago and the sight of million-dollar yachts. Normally, this is a place where wealthy people unwind to the sound of lapping waves or enjoy a cool drink in the hotel's 30m-long bar. However, Lars and the rest of the team must abstain from alcoholic drinks ahead of the semi-final. But for Lars, it's not a great sacrifice. He spends most of the preparation time playing whist with defender Torben Piechnik and midfielder Johnny Mølby.

Leading up to the semi-final, Lars can clearly sense the increased interest in him. This includes the Dutch press, who know that he speaks Dutch and remember him from his time at Feyenoord.

The encounter with the country where he had two difficult years provides motivation for Lars, who feels that he has something to prove. Not because he knows the current Dutch national team players personally, but he knows that his old colleagues are watching. Joop Hiele, Sjaak Troost, Regi Blinker, Simon Tahamata, coach Rinus Israel, and especially all the Feyenoord fans who blamed him for the team's failure. Those who labelled him a disappointment and a bad purchase. He knows that the journalists who wrote that he wasn't worth the money will be reporting from the match or watching it on TV.

Much has happened since Lars left Feyenoord. The four years in Odense and Luton have changed him, and he is better, faster, and mentally stronger than when he played in the Netherlands. He has gained a lot of experience, and the recent experience of success surrounds him like a golden aura.

It's not that he is filled with a thirst for revenge. And he doesn't see himself as a victim. He knows that the problems at Feyenoord were as much a result of his own struggles as they were the result of his surroundings. Other, mentally stronger individuals might have thrived with the competitive mentality that existed in a top professional league such as the Eredivisie. Moreover, seeking revenge is not in Lars's nature. However, he still feels that there is something 'unresolved' from his time at Feyenoord. He left the club without truly being able to showcase his abilities. It's unsatisfying for a person who wants to contribute and has had success everywhere except Feyenoord: IF Fjorden, Randers Freja, Brøndby IF, OB, Luton Town, OB again, and the Danish national team.

And 24 hours before the semi-final, he shows that he is more mentally prepared than ever.

Lars Elstrup is ready

During the tactical meeting the day before the semi-finals, Richard Møller Nielsen discusses all possible scenarios that may occur in the match. This includes extra time and a possible penalty shoot-out.

'Who will be ready to take penalties?' Ricardo asks his players. He naturally pays attention to those who are penalty takers for their clubs, but he wants the players to volunteer themselves. And

Lars is both: a penalty taker for OB and very clear in his response. He immediately agrees to take one if needed.

Lars has taken several penalties for his clubs in Denmark, the Netherlands, and England, and knows that he is a reliable shooter. The relaxed atmosphere helps him step forward and take responsibility.

'I wasn't nervous about taking the penalty because the atmosphere within the team had been relaxed throughout the entire European Championship due to the lack of high expectations on us. And before the semi-final, we were still a bunch of happy boys who just wanted to do our best,' he says.

'There was really this feeling that if someone were to miss a penalty, it would be OK.'

In the first 57 minutes, Lars is not close to the penalty spot. Ricardo sticks to his preferred combination of Povlsen and Brian Laudrup up front. Lars is the preferred attacking substitute.

And it becomes necessary when the lightweight and technical Brian Laudrup starts feeling the strain of the intense European Championship schedule after a season of Bundesliga football with Bayern Munich. He can only last for about an hour, but he has challenged the Dutch team and been involved in setting up Henrik Larsen's two goals, making 'Store' the tournament's top scorer.

Lars enters the field, but with a different role and much more playing time than against France. Denmark are leading 2-1, and Lars's role primarily involves being the first defender to pressurise the increasingly time-pressed Dutch players. But four minutes before the end of regular time, the Netherlands equalise after a corner, putting Denmark to a physical and mental test.

Extra time becomes a gruelling battle to hold on to the draw until what appears to be Denmark's best chance for a place in the final arrives: the penalty shoot-out.

And they make it. Inside the centre circle, Ricardo and his assistants approach the players who have already been designated as takers to check their current condition and make sure they are ready.

'I answered, "Yes, if I can take the third penalty," because three was my lucky number,' Lars explains.

'I didn't want to take the first or last penalty – three suited me fine.'

Decisive intuition

As the third shooter, Lars also has the opportunity to watch five penalties. Three from the Netherlands, two from Denmark, and then it's his turn. Central defender Ronald Koeman starts with a successful shot for the defending European champions, followed by the confident Larsen, who equalises.

Then two dramatic moments occur. First, the 1988 European Championship star Marco van Basten misses his penalty – or rather, Peter Schmeichel dives the right way and saves his shot.

Denmark can take the lead. But the Netherlands also have a goalkeeper with match-winning experience. The charismatic veteran Hans van Breukelen is notorious for psyching out penalty takers and often succeeds. Van Breukelen has one of the highest penalty-saving percentages and four years prior, he saved one in the European Championship Final against the Soviet Union.

Van Breukelen tries to distract Povlsen with some small talk inside the penalty box. Povlsen pushes the provocative goalkeeper away, but back on the goal line, van Breukelen comes close to fulfilling his intention. Povlsen strikes his shot hard to one side, and van Breukelen dives in the same direction but only manages to graze the ball with his hand. Povlsen clenches his hands together in extreme relief and triumph. Denmark are still ahead by one.

Dennis Bergkamp keeps the Netherlands level at 2-2, putting the pressure on Lars. If he misses, the teams will be even after the same amount of kicks, and the Netherlands' next taker – Frank Rijkaard, whose goal after 86 minutes of normal time made the score 2-2 – can give his team the upper hand.

But first, Lars has to take his penalty. He is familiar with van Breukelen, who knows that Lars speaks Dutch.

'I had seen what happened with the previous penalty, and Flemming Povlsen tackled van Breukelen in his own way. He maintained his focus and concentration and took his shot as he had to,' Lars recalls.

'And when it was my turn, I thought that I shouldn't engage in a discussion with van Breukelen, so I wanted to keep my distance from him. And if he had come off his line, I would have stopped, stepped back, and let the referee bring him back on to the line.

'So I just wanted to let him do his show and try to maintain my focus. And that's what I did.'

Lars is not the kind of penalty taker who watches the goalkeeper, waits for his movement, and places the ball accordingly. He makes the decision in advance, and it unfolds as planned.

'I'm the one who makes the decision in advance and then executes my shot. I'm conservative, stuck in my ways, relying on my shot and technique,' he explains. In his preparation, he decides not to follow the advice he received as a child playing football in Jutland.

'My father always said that I should kick the ball to the right side, half a metre off the ground. That's how you should take a penalty,' Lars says.

'But my thoughts were that as a left-footed player, I should shoot to the left side of the goal with the inside of my foot. And hard. Either along the ground or high into the top corner, but outside the goalkeeper's reach.

'That's what I had to do, that was my firm decision.'

Lars maintains his composure throughout the long, lonely walk from the centre circle to the penalty spot. He steps forward towards the ball. Van Breukelen stands on the goal line, as he should. He blows on his fingertips, lightly hops on his feet, preparing himself.

A crowd of 37,450 in the stands, including 3,000 Danes, and millions of viewers worldwide watch with anticipation as the timid boy from Råby, wearing the number ten, prepares to take his shot. He takes a solid five or six strides of a run-up and strikes the ball. Van Breukelen leans towards the left and dives in the exact direction where Lars had planned to place the ball, but the Dutch goalkeeper dives in vain. The ball whizzes into the top corner of the net, just about in the middle of the goal, slightly towards the right side and about half a metre off the ground. Van Breukelen lies halfway in the grass, covering the left side that Lars had chosen.

'At the moment of the shot or just a split second before, I change my decision and shoot the opposite way, for the first and only time in my entire career,' Lars reveals.

'Afterwards, it looks like a sure goal, but if I hadn't changed my mind at the last moment, I would have shot to the side where van Breukelen dived and he would have saved it.'

A decisive intuitive moment in Lars's continued momentum of success. It's completed by Kim Vilfort and Kim Christofte, who respond to two further Dutch goals, securing Denmark a sensational place in the European Championship Final.

The team that wasn't even supposed to be in the tournament will now play in the final. And they will face the Germans, who defeated the hosts in Stockholm the day before and had already booked their return tickets for the day after the final.

There are four days until the final, and right now, Denmark is boiling over with excitement. The celebrations of the semi-final victory turn inner Copenhagen and the country's main streets into veritable party venues in the bright midsummer night. Good luck to everyone.

The darkness sets in

The nation is in a state of collective ecstasy and wants more, and the sports press covers the event extensively. But for Lars, a transformation occurs, as sudden as it is overwhelming. Dark thoughts are once again penetrating his mind.

'There was suddenly a shift from the previous games where I felt ready to play, felt I had good legs, and felt good enough. And it happened during the four days between the semi-final and the final against Germany,' says Lars.

He cannot pinpoint exactly when the gloom clouds his mind. During a night's sleep in the luxurious yacht hotel? While having breakfast in the restaurant? Under the shower after a training session? Out on the training field? He doesn't know. He just feels it as it is: utterly overwhelming and darkening. And he can feel that it radically disrupts his mental balance. For Lars, the match against Germany will remain a sad and hazy memory of the horror and fear that have often plagued him. But it happens right in the middle of the greatest triumph ever experienced by the Danish national team. A football match watched by virtually the entire Danish population and millions of football enthusiasts worldwide.

The final for the European Championship has not yet kicked off, but for Lars, it's already over.

Whereas Lars has been frustrated in previous matches for not getting the chance to start, he now feels relieved when the coach announces the starting line-up with Povlsen and Brian Laudrup up top. Lars is fortunately relegated to the bench. And that's exactly where he wants to be when he has to be present at the stadium. Far enough away from the centre of events. Not involved in the greatest sports event in Danish history. On the bench, he still feels the intrusive anxiety of making sudden mistakes. But on the bench, he cannot make those mistakes. And nobody is looking at him. All eyes are focused on the game on the field. And he's not there. And hopefully, he won't have to be.

For Lars, it's all just the same. He doesn't care about the result of the match right now. He doesn't have the energy or focus for it. The only thing that matters to him is to stay safely on the bench.

'I really don't care if we win or lose, as long as I don't have to go on the field,' he says. 'And I'm afraid that we'll fall behind because then I might have to go on the field, just like against France.'

But Lars doesn't have to worry about that. His former teammate from Brøndby, John 'Faxe' Jensen, puts Denmark in the lead after 18 minutes with his legendary long shot.

The Germans press and press, and Schmeichel and his defence have to resort to all kinds of manoeuvres to fend off the impending equaliser. It's all about defence now. Lars doesn't feel good, but he can breathe just a little easier. And even more so when Vilfort, in the 79th minute, holds off two Germans in a counterattack and shoots the ball low into the net via the post. Flemming Toft, the commentator, lets out a loud 'hutlihut', a nonsensical word that has since become a part of the Danish vocabulary. Denmark are leading 2-0, with a measly 12 minutes remaining.

Photographer: Bax Lindhardt

1981, with Randers Freja in Mallorca. In the background, you can see the idol, national team player Per Røntved. Photographer: Private

1988, the Elstrup family in Råby during one of the happy moments, while the family idyll was still intact. Photographer: Private

1990, Elstrup for Luton before a game vs Crystal Palace away.

1991, Elstrup for Luton vs Aston Villa, at Villa Park; League Division One.

1992, Elstrup celebrates with Sivebaek and Christofte, after beating France in Euro 92. Photographer: WEREK Pressebildagentur/Süddeutsche Zeitung Photo

2000, Elstrup with blue rope and roller skates on the pedestrian street in Odense.
Photographer: Wilmann Thomas

2011, Elstrup on his boat in the harbour.
Photographer: Bax Lindhardt

The victory is almost secured. All that remains for Denmark is to maintain their defensive and destructive discipline against the increasingly resigned Germans. For that purpose, Denmark's creative and goalscoring number ten requires no effort, and that fact warms his heart. It's his personal joy. His inner *hutlihut*.

The subsequent celebrations in the seconds and minutes after the final whistle are of historical magnitude for Denmark. But for Lars, the scenes of celebration, the presentation of the European Championship trophy, and the lap of honour are things to be endured.

Lars's emotions are in an almost absurd contrast to what surrounds him. Victorious Danish players, the coach, and team managers, and ecstatic and happy fans in the stands. UEFA's Swedish president, Lennart Johansson, proclaims Denmark as 'EUROPEAN CHAMPIONS 1992' over the loudspeakers, and captain Lars Olsen and later the other players proudly lift the trophy amid a rain of camera flashes. The stadium explodes in more jubilant outbursts.

'Just after the match ended, I thought I should sneak down to the group of celebrating players,' Elstrup says as he begins his recollection.

'And then we went on a victory lap, where Schmeichel was out at the fence to celebrate with the travelling Danish fans. I continued to sneak around, chatted a bit with the other substitutes, but I couldn't show any particular joy.

'When we received the trophy, Flemming Povlsen stood there and cried with happiness. But I positioned myself at the back with the others who hadn't played much or at all.

'Actually, I just wanted to go back to the hotel, where I could feel safe.'

The day after

At the team hotel, Lars has to wait a while before he can go to bed. Richard Møller Nielsen acts as the lead singer in several cheerful songs, and the players sing along, including Lars. He maintains his facade, smiles, celebrates, and drinks along with the others. He feels a great sense of relief when he finally retires to his room. He is eager to start his vacation, ready to get away.

However, he has to wait a little longer. The day after, the squad is transported back to Copenhagen, where over 100,000 Danes wait to celebrate with the team on Rådhuspladsen (City Hall Square). The journey from Kastrup Airport is a true and unforgettable triumph, with the players being applauded everywhere they go on the open-top bus.

On the flight from Gothenburg's Landvetter Airport, Lars begins to relax a little. He is handed a can of beer, and just before the landing at Kastrup, he and his team-mates enjoy the reception from the air force: two F16 fighters, whose pilots are wearing the classic caps of that time.

The players are hailed as heroes, and the triumph in the European Championship comes with a series of gifts. In addition to a generous victory bonus from the Danish Football Association, the team's apparel manufacturer, Hummel, has gifted each player a holiday trip with a companion. Furthermore, the team's final hotel in Stenungsund has offered each player an all-expenses-paid weekend getaway for two. One of the more amusing gifts comes from a Scottish whisky company, which offers each player a case of whisky if they come to collect it themselves. Like the rest of the players, Lars has no idea how he will get 12 bottles of whisky through customs!

First and foremost, Lars must try to get through the day with the nationally televised tribute. He positions himself at the back of the bus, with Schmeichel at the front wearing a police cap. He receives another beer and then another one, while the bus slowly rolls through the sea of people on Amager towards Rådhuspladsen. It moves so slowly that Lars and other players actually have time to jump off the bus, take care of their needs at a cafe or another suitable place, and then jump back on board.

There, he drinks another beer, toasts, and cheers, even though he just wants to get away. However, nobody can sense or see that in him. They see a Danish European Championship hero who, like the other players, lets go, celebrates, and basks in the adoration.

'It eased the situation a bit when I had a couple of beers. And it also helped that the final was now far enough away. That made it a little easier,' Lars says about the big tribute day.

'Besides the beers, I had also received a Danish flag, so I had something to hold on to during the reception at the city hall.'

'And I also had the courage to step out on to the city hall balcony a few times and look out over the jubilant crowd.'

Today, he has no difficulty recognising the historic triumph that the European Championship gold was and all the pride and joy that came with the victory.

'And the joy has been just as great and justified among all those who watched the final at the stadium or on TV as it was among us players,' he recalls. 'I don't see any difference.'

But Lars himself didn't feel good that day. He just didn't.

A glimpse of Lars Elstrup

Later that summer, Lars returns home to his childhood town of Råby to relax and spend some time with his parents. Naturally, European Championship fever has also been running high in

Lars's hometown. Tage and Ingelise have received congratulations from near and far, and even the director of the United Danish Consumers' Cooperative Society has sent a greeting to the manager of the Cooperative in Råby.

Tage and Ingelise beam with pride every time someone congratulates them on their son's European Championship win. Like the rest of Denmark, they find it difficult to comprehend that Denmark are truly the European champions, but it is even harder for them to understand that their son has played a significant role in it.

It was something that Tage could hardly dare to dream about when he saw his son kicking a ball in the backyard. But in that way, he also feels that he has a small share in the success. It was him who helped Lars eliminate his mistakes, become better, more focused, and above all, have the will to succeed. It is that will that has now made him a European champion.

The enthusiasm is also great among the excited football youth of Råby when Lars shows up to a barbecue wearing the national team's training gear in July 1992. The occasion is the inauguration of a new 'football field' for the children in his childhood neighbourhood.

Despite its modest size and appearance, this patch of grass has been the backdrop for many football matches over the years. And on this warm summer evening, a European champion himself joins one of the teams. Adjusting to the level of the younger opponents, Lars enthusiastically engages in duels and gives 'everything he's got', to the delight of the young lads, including Christian Degn, the boy who received a Christmas card from Lars a few years earlier while he was playing in England.

Christian is now 12 years old, and Lars is still his great idol. The success at Euro '92 hasn't changed that. Today, Christian vividly remembers that particular barbecue and friendly match in the summer of 1992, where an unfortunate incident led him to give his idol the nickname 'The Chicken Killer'.

'We were playing this football match, and suddenly Lars shoots a hard shot. Unfortunately for him, the ball goes straight into a nearby chicken coop and hits a chicken, which drops dead,' explains Christian.

Just like the accidental burning of the field in the summer of 1975, Lars's 'chicken murder' was also unintentional.

However, that is not the event that Christian primarily recalls many years later. Instead, it is the exchange of words he had with his football hero during a brief moment alone with him, as someone he admires and looks up to.

Naturally, Christian has followed Lars throughout the entire European Championship, and like any other football-interested boy, he has dreamed of playing in a Euro final himself. Christian has empathised with Elstrup over his bench position in the final. And now, with his idol in Råby, he can appropriately ask him his burning question: wasn't it frustrating to sit on the bench in the final?

The curious young lad expects to have his investigative enquiry honoured with answers like 'Yes, you bet it was frustrating' or 'Yes, but I was still glad we won!'

But the answer that Lars provides is unexpected and shakes the boy's understanding of his football hero and the world of playing stars that he himself dreams of being a part of.

Lars looks at him and responds, 'No, because I actually didn't want to play at all. I was afraid of coming on to the field and making a mistake.'

It is a refreshing glimpse of honesty from Lars, who otherwise has not made an effort to open up and show his true feelings to anyone. In this brief conversation with a young boy from his childhood neighbourhood, Lars reveals a glimpse of something that the world is not yet aware of. But soon it will be.

11
Anxiety

IN JUNE 1993, a special episode takes place during the national team's training before the World Cup qualifying match against Albania.

'We are finishing the last training session in Vedbæk the day before the important match at Parken [Idrætsparken]. At one point, I go out to take a corner kick, and as I kick, I feel a little snap in my left inner thigh,' Lars explains.

'Shortly after, we get another corner kick. I know within myself that if I take one more kick, I will get a pulled muscle and won't be able to play the game the next day. I think about it for a moment, and then I take the kick.'

The fear of not performing has now become so great that Lars is willing to harm himself to avoid playing. That's why he takes the kick. The fear of playing has simply become greater than the fear of the pain that naturally comes with an injury. But Elstrup doesn't care. There's nothing else to do, as he sees it.

In his football world, it is not an option to say, 'I'm not playing tomorrow because I'm afraid of making mistakes!'

It is also not a real possibility to talk about performance anxiety and other mental problems. Not for Lars, who has never shared his innermost thoughts and worries with anyone.

Grateful duty

Most people would probably think that he should be grateful. He plays for the national team, every football boy's dream, and he is selected for a World Cup qualifying match in the national arena. But a packed Idrætsparken is the last place Lars wants to perform right now. He is scared. But he can't tell the coaching staff. It's easier to get a pulled muscle. That's completely understandable. Something everyone can comprehend. Of course, it will disappoint the coach that Lars has to withdraw from another international match, and the press may wonder why he is injured again. But it doesn't matter what they think. He is injured now, and nothing can be said or done about it.

Recently, Lars's performance anxiety has worsened. That wasn't the plan when he returned to OB the year before. He has come home as a star, and his performance in the European Championship has only increased his popularity. He commands respect from team-mates and opponents alike, and many believe that Lars is too good to play for a Danish club. But that's not how he sees it. Even though he smiles and says that he is doing well and enjoys playing, his inner self feels like a ticking bomb just waiting to explode.

The success of the national team at the Euros has led to increased interest in its players, and several secure lucrative contracts. For example, Brian Laudrup moves to Italian club Fiorentina, John Sivebæk to Italian club Pescara, and John Jensen to Arsenal. There is also interest in Lars, but he stays where he is. He has returned to OB to initiate the career break he has long desired.

In the days following the Euro final, when confronted with interest from foreign clubs, he jokes in *Ekstra Bladet* that he is not interested in a move 'unless Real Madrid want me', knowing perfectly well that the Spanish giants are unlikely to pursue him.

At the same time, OB's director, Jørgen Bækkelund, also rejects the idea of selling Lars. In the new 1992/93 season, the club is in a much better financial position, and this time intends to maintain its place in the Superliga and even compete for the top spots.

When his contract expires the following year, Lars can leave quite cheaply. But it's a risk Bækkelund is willing to take, partly because he expects Elstrup to be persuaded to sign a new contract and partly because Lars himself has made it clear that he doesn't want to move abroad.

The invisible plague

Anxiety is going to grow during Lars's last year as a professional footballer. But it's not visible in him when he starts the season after the Euro finals.

In early September 1992, the prominent French sports magazine *L'Équipe* is present at Odense Stadium to do a report on the man who knocked France out of the Euros but usually plays in more humble settings. The journalist has something to report as Lars plays a dream game and scores one of the best goals of his career in the 5-0 victory against BK Frem.

The goal comes just as Richard Møller Nielsen is about to announce the squad for the prestigious match against Germany. Moreover, the game marks the opening of the newly renovated Idrætsparken, now an all-seater stadium.

Lars assumes he will start on the bench, so after the successful match against Frem, he cheekily says to the journalists, 'What the hell does it take to start? Do I have to score five times?' Lars rarely highlights himself, but a creeping change can be detected.

Before the goalless World Cup qualifier against Latvia the week before, he makes it clear that, despite being labelled 'the world's best joker', he is tired of being on the bench.

Currently, he is the top scorer in the Superliga, and against the Germans he is allowed to start. He rewards this opportunity by equalising at 1-1 with nine minutes remaining. However, the game ends in German revenge, but at a time when there is a lack of goalscorers Lars shows that he is still the man who stands in the right place at the right time.

The goal is his 13th in 26 internationals. Impressive; one every other game, but the goal will also turn out to be Elstrup's last for Denmark. Both at OB and the national team, he gradually assumes a more withdrawn role on the field: a partial but far from satisfying explanation for his decreasing goal tally.

Far worse than the lack of international goals and the reduced goalscoring in OB's shirt is that performance anxiety has truly started to grow behind the star's facade. Despite playing well for OB in the autumn of 1992 and continuing to do so in the spring season of 1993, he doesn't feel well.

'I came back to OB to find peace and maybe have a couple of good years where I could rediscover the joy of football before retiring,' Lars states, adding quietly, 'But it just didn't happen.'

Contempt for personal welfare and self-destruction

On the field, the anxiety is expressed in a playing style that leads him to seek confrontation. Perhaps to gain the recognition of his team-mates and fans, but also in a form of bizarre contempt for his own safety. As if there is an implicit desire to get injured in his playing style, thus avoiding the two-headed monster: the game of football and performance anxiety.

In the spring of 1993, when OB visit the Brøndby Stadium, Lars sees a cross that lands in the open space between himself and home goalkeeper Mogens Krogh. Instinctively, Lars knows that he must sacrifice himself to win the duel against Krogh, who is one of his card game friends from the national team. Lars throws himself towards the ball without any real expectation of reaching it. And then the inevitable happens: he collides with Krogh with a crash, feels the pain, and doesn't remember anything else. Lars is knocked unconscious and has to be carried off the field.

'To reach the ball, I had to sacrifice myself, and I did, without thinking about the consequences. And then it's no longer fun,' he recalls.

And indeed, it was no longer fun with the national team either, cemented by the infamous training session before the match against Albania, where Lars consciously inflicts harm upon himself.

Just two months prior, Lars received great praise for his performance in an away match against Ireland, which ended in a 1-1 draw. The legendary Per Høyer Hansen writes in *Tipsbladet* about what will turn out to be Lars's last international match, '[Elstrup] became a kind of symbol of the Danish team's fighting spirit because he fought throughout the match, both in midfield and as a striker. He handled this double role impressively. He was strong in duels and pushed the ball forward. His herculean effort cost him energy, and even though Elstrup didn't score this time, it was one of his best international matches.'

He is still a competent national team player, but mentally he can't handle it any more. The pulled muscle from the corner in Vedbæk only confirms what he has long sensed but has not yet acted upon: he must quit before things go completely wrong.

And it's precisely then that he truly realises that he has postponed the decision for far too long. It's a drastic step to resort to self-destructive actions because where is the limit? What will he do next to avoid a football match?

But he can't just quit now. Can't he handle the last few matches with OB? And he can probably resist the expected pressure around him for more. OB have long wanted to renew his expiring contract. But Lars has alternately rejected them or postponed the discussion, saying that he will 'think about it'. But now he knows that he won't renew. He doesn't want to any more.

Elstrup quits

In May 1993, Lars helps secure a 2-0 victory for OB in the cup final against AaB. He scores from a penalty and assists in the second goal. Shortly after, when OB secure the runners-up spot in the Danish championship, Lars also plays his last match at the top level. Ten days after the end of the season, his press release arrives at editorial offices throughout the country.

'The last impression is always the strongest. I'm quitting now while things are good. I want to be remembered for something positive. I won't jeopardise that by continuing now and becoming a laughing stock. I made the decision myself. The doctors didn't pressure me. I could have continued.

'I've had back problems, a groin injury, and some meniscus flaps have been removed from my knee. I wasn't able to play at a satisfactory level any more,' says Lars as he announces his retirement at the end of June 1993. Only he knows the deeper reason for ending his career.

Reactions from fans, media, and team-mates are filled with regret and words of praise for the player and the man. Most are sorry to lose one of the league's and the national team's great names but also express respect for Elstrup's choice. Richard Møller Nielsen tells *Ekstra Bladet*, 'It's a shame for Lars, who had an ability that isn't found very often, simply a goalscoring instinct, and he was a versatile and effective player who performed well both in midfield and as a striker … As one of the veterans, he was an important part of the collective and a good team-mate.'

Although the coach is saddened to lose a player with 13 goals in 34 international matches, he expresses respect for the decision, 'Lars has been 100 per cent honest when he has had to withdraw from the team, which unfortunately he has had to do a couple of times. As soon as he wasn't ready, he withdrew instead of going on to the field with injuries. That's sensible. The body has to last a lifetime.'

OB director Jørgen Bækkelund, who has long sought to extend Lars's contract, also expresses his regret. He knows Lars well enough to know that the decision is final but adds that he will always be welcome back at OB.

'It's a significant loss for the club. In addition to being a valuable and very dangerous player, he also had a big influence, especially on the young players in the club. On and off the field, he spent a lot of time helping the young players, and that characterises a great personality that is difficult to replace,' Bækkelund tells *Ekstra Bladet* on 22 June.

Although Lars had a different perception of his role, he is aware that his inner struggle has not been visible to others. He has been afraid to go to training and meet his team-mates, who see him as a leader and a role model. The contrast between Lars's self-image and his team-mates' image of him is complete. But considering the situation, it's quite convenient that only Lars himself knows how he has truly felt.

He still refuses to comment on the decision and rejects several offers for exclusive interviews. Lars has bid farewell and explained himself.

12

Sangha and the New Life

FOR THE first time in many years, Lars Elstrup can enjoy a summer vacation without having to worry about staying in shape and maintaining his weight. He visits his parents in Råby briefly, but primarily he stays at his in-laws' summer house in Hasmark, on the northern part of the island of Funen. He is with his girlfriend Charlotte. They enjoy each other's company, delighting in their holiday and free time. They also discuss the possibility of expanding their family. They have known each other for four years now, and having children feels like a natural next step. And now, since Lars has ended his football career, they have even more time for it.

Financially, they have no concerns, and space is not an issue either. There is plenty of room in their large apartment on Dronningensgade.

But Lars has other, darker thoughts occupying his mind.

Explosion in the summer paradise

In the beautiful summer landscape of Funen, the beer is cold and refreshing, the waves are blue, the days are warm, and the evenings are bright.

The coveted free space is right there, and for the first time in his life, Lars is in a situation where he doesn't have to do what others expect of him. But instead of feeling peaceful, Lars realises that he still doesn't feel good about himself. Instead of diminishing, his anxiety attacks have intensified, as have his bouts of depression. He often lies on the sofa all day, unable to get up, lacking the strength to face the day.

As summer comes to an end and the football season starts again, he may be relieved not to be part of the pressure associated with matches and training any more. But his thoughts are still filled with unrest. Gradually, he realises that what he needs is not a vacation or free time. He craves something deeper, something existential. Even though he had a good long holiday with Charlotte, he still feels drained of energy. He still can't handle anything and, above all, feels that something is missing in his life. He begins to realise that he needs more than just a physical break; he needs something much deeper. Something that can't be achieved by taking time off or escaping life's challenges.

'It's like blowing up a balloon, at some point it will explode. And that's what happened to me in 1993 when all my anxieties about what was expected of me culminated,' reflects Lars on that period in the late summer of 1993, when he started taking his inner longing seriously.

'I didn't know what to do, and in reality, I was just living a superficial life, where only one or two per cent of me was truly alive.

'Just as people may need to go on vacation, travel around the world, or take a sabbatical and get away from it all, they can also need to find inner peace.

'Everyone has that desire, but it's not enough to simply go on a physical vacation; you also need to find that space within yourself.'

Since returning to Odense, Lars has sporadically taken his spiritual quest seriously. He has attended services at Råby Church on several Sundays and listened to the priest's sermons. He has read a couple of profound books. He has also discussed the meaning of life in conversations with his friend and colleague Lars Høgh. However, it has never gone deeper than questions like 'Is there life in outer space?' or 'What happens when we die?'

Lars's spiritual interest has not gone unnoticed by his team-mates either. When he turns 30 in March 1993, he receives the book *De Store Filosoffer* (The Great Philosophers) as a gift from coach Kim Brink and his team-mates. He has read the book since, but hasn't found the meaning of life in it.

But he continues his search. And even more so after his football career ends.

A random trip, a radical life change

One random day, Lars takes a casual stroll through the town when his attention is suddenly caught by a brochure for a self-development course at a health food store. He takes the brochure and reads it. The course is supposed to last for 14 days, takes place on a farm in the Odense area, and is organised by Sangha, a new religious movement derived from the Wild Goose Company. This organisation was founded by British lawyer and guru Michael Barnett, who was originally a disciple of the Indian Bhagwan movement led by guru Bhagwan Rajneesh. Barnett has his headquarters in a castle in France but has branches all over Europe, where he stays, teaches, and holds meetings with local leaders.

Sangha is led by the couple Hubbi Heiming and Knud Kløvedal. They met in the late 1980s at a meditation course and then moved to Funen, where they started teaching people in crisis. They work based on various religious and therapeutic approaches, including meditation, healing, rebirthing, kinesiology, and talk therapy. Knud is one of the residents of the famous 1960s commune Maos Lyst, where the well-known sailor and author Troels Kløvedal and the late social commentator Ebbe Kløvedal also live. The residents took the surname Kløvedal from a location in J.R.R. Tolkien's masterpiece *The Lord of the Rings*.

Sangha formulates its purpose as follows, 'We see the planet Earth at a crossroads, where each of us can live in harmony and respectful attention with the Earth, or where we make the Earth uninhabitable for us humans by denying ourselves.'

The way they achieve this is defined as follows, 'In a safe and relaxed atmosphere, the daily work of cleaning, cooking, laundry, and property maintenance becomes the starting point for working on oneself.'

Lars doesn't know much about all this when he decides to attend the course. He has already begun his spiritual quest, and he is simply curious, open, and hoping for some interesting and rewarding weeks on the course.

The course will prove to touch something deep within him in several ways.

Challenging thoughts

First and foremost, Lars likes the idea of working on himself. And the thoughts of liberation, which the course primarily focuses on, resonate with his strong desire for freedom. He has longed to be free. Free from performance anxiety. Free from the inability to speak up and assert himself. Free to exist. Free to be himself. Free to feel the zest for life. Something he hasn't experienced in other contexts.

'On that course, I felt seen, heard, and understood, and I found joy there,' he says today.

'It was very unfamiliar for me to talk about some of the things I discussed. But I could do it there, which was a relief in itself. Because if you don't talk about things, you keep it all inside, and then you become a ticking bomb.

'Besides, I was with others who shared my mindset, and I realised that I wasn't the only one with problems.'

On the course, Lars is introduced to meditation and various therapeutic exercises. And simply put, he learns to open up to other people. In this case, two course leaders and around 18 other participants. This requires a tremendous personal effort.

'Just the fact that I had to stand there and hold another person's hand could make me break out in a sweat. And I was on the verge of having a panic attack when I had to share something in a large gathering, something more intimate about myself,' he recalls.

'So it was certainly challenging but also new and exciting.'

Lars especially feels the benefit of 'opening up more and going beyond one's own insecurities and anxieties to discover other and more aspects of oneself'.

After completing the first part of the course, Hubbi Heiming presents Lars with an interesting opportunity. She suggests that he can move into Sangha's collective living arrangement just outside Odense. Lars is taken aback by the idea. He has benefited from the course so far, and he has enjoyed meeting these open and attentive people. But moving in?

It's a challenging thought, but he isn't dismissive. Perhaps it's precisely what he needs? Perhaps only by moving away from his familiar environment can he truly find peace? He carefully considers Hubbi's offer.

The idea appeals to him, but the decision requires courage. Charlotte will be upset, and his family will be puzzled. His father probably won't understand why Lars's life is about spiritual growth in a collective living arrangement.

But Lars feels that he has done things for others long enough and not according to his own desires. After a Sunday lunch at Sangha, he decides to move into the collective.

He has experienced various uncertain football adventures, but this decision seems to be the most drastic of his life.

Break-up with Charlotte

Lars is completely determined when he shares his plans to move with Charlotte. The decision is his and cannot be changed. Now, he just needs to deal with the practical aspects. And he needs to break up with his girlfriend.

'I had decided to move, and it wasn't something I was ready to discuss,' he says.

'The decision was impulsive. So once I knew what I wanted, it was just a matter of doing it.'

Understandably, Charlotte reacts strongly to Lars's sudden announcement. She has noticed that he has been quite melancholic at times, but they have been doing well together. They have known each other for many years, and they have shared experiences that she believed had brought them closer.

She had no sense that there were any issues in their relationship or that Lars was considering leaving her. She is deeply shocked by his decision.

'She became very upset and couldn't understand why I wanted to move there because she saw our life together differently than I did. She thought we were doing great,' says Lars.

'The break-up didn't feel hard for me; it was more like a relief because I had made up my mind that I wanted to move into the collective.'

Lars packs a few things and leaves Charlotte and their apartment. He also feels that he is leaving behind his old life. When he quit football, he thought it might help him feel better. But now he realises that something much more drastic is needed if he is to move forward in his life. Despite the significant personal costs and deeply hurting Charlotte, he believes that these choices are necessary.

'For the first time in my life, I did something without considering what others thought. And I was completely clear about that,' says Lars.

Voluntary isolation

With a clear mind, Lars moves to Sangha's property in Højby, 10km (6 miles) south-east of Odense, on 1 October 1993. The collective consists of a series of caravans where the approximately 40 residents have their own rooms but share bathroom facilities, kitchen, and a couple of common living rooms in the adjacent half-timbered house.

Thus, the 174-square-metre apartment in Odense city centre is replaced by a new existence in a small 14-square-metre caravan. The rent is slightly cheaper, though. He pays 2,200 kroner (£250), and an additional 1,100 kroner is required for monthly food expenses. It's a different situation, but it doesn't bother him.

'We had filled the Odense apartment with material possessions: a large TV, expensive furniture, and so on. But it wasn't something that made me happier,' Lars says.

On the same evening he bids farewell to Charlotte, he lies on the bed in the small caravan. He has unpacked his few belongings and contemplates the enormous decision he has made. But he feels relieved and on his way to something better.

The other residents of the collective welcome him politely. Some know him from his football days, while others have no idea who he is. But it doesn't matter. In Sangha, there may be a couple of spiritual leaders, but no football stars.

Formally, both Hubbi and Knud are leaders of the place, but Lars quickly senses that Hubbi is the undisputed authority. She had also shown a special interest in Lars when he first appeared at the self-development course. Hubbi is charismatic, and there is an allure about her that leaves an impression on Lars. He appreciates her advances and a relationship begins.

Shortly after his arrival, she presents Lars with an unexpected challenge. 'I agreed with Hubbi that for the first 14 days, I wouldn't talk to anyone "out in the world", meaning family and friends. It was supposed to be a kind of exercise,' he explains.

'And it was exciting, something I hadn't tried or heard of before. It was like a tennis coach telling his student, "Try hitting 20 backhand shots so you become good at it!" In the same way, I found this exercise interesting in being able to focus on myself.

'Besides, I didn't feel like talking to anyone from the outside. That's what I wanted to get away from.'

The exercise is about granting him peace from the surroundings that have demanded so much from him for so long. Fourteen days of complete tranquillity without external influence. Lars is comfortable with it, and he feels that Hubbi, for the second time in the three weeks he has known her, understands him better than the people he has known for years. The first time, she showed him that it was OK to be unsure and afraid, and now she understands that what he needs the most is peace and tranquillity.

He feels accepted and understood by her, and that makes him trust the suggestions she comes up with.

The external environment

While Lars finds this new world exciting and challenging, he has left his parents and girlfriend in shock and disbelief. 'Initially, we didn't think it was that bad with him,' mother Ingelise says today, and father Tage adds, 'But then we started to fear the worst and went to the collective.' Upon their arrival at Sangha, they meet a quiet Lars, who briefly breaks his isolation period to greet them. He seems OK with their presence. After a tour of the collective and some polite pleasantries, Ingelise gets straight to the point when she and her son stand at the gate, smoking a cigarette.

'Now, are you sure this isn't like Scientology?' she asks with concern.

'Yes,' Lars answers, takes a drag of the cigarette, and laughs awkwardly. He's not lying. He knows it's not like Scientology, and he hasn't experienced anything he dislikes. If it's a sect, it's far less frightening than what such things are often made out to be.

However, his words have far from convinced his parents, and the atmosphere in the car is sombre as Ingelise and Tage drive back to Råby. Tage, the more sceptical of the parents, is convinced that Sangha is not a place he wants to visit frequently. Instead, he hopes to convince his son of the foolishness of his choice of residence.

Before they leave, Tage looks Lars in the eyes and says, 'I have a feeling I'll never see you again!'

It's not meant as a threat or an accusation. It's a father's honest concern for the son he's afraid of losing. 'You'll never get out of there,' he tries again. Tage is far from the strong, authoritative father that Lars remembers. Instead, he sees a worried old man who desperately hopes to make his son regret his decision.

Tage feels like he might be bidding farewell to the son he has known for over 30 years. Ingelise feels the same way but still chooses to maintain contact with Lars as much as possible.

Angry and reclusive

When the media learn that Lars has moved into a spiritual collective, they react with disbelief. But they also have a keen sense for a good story. A football star joining a 'religious sect' a year and a half after winning the European Championship sells newspapers.

Ekstra Bladet splashes the headline 'Elstrup's Sex Guru' across most of the front page, and several team-mates express their bewilderment about his new life. Some journalists even venture to visit Lars in hopes of getting an exclusive interview and insight into the former football star's new life. Lars is dismissive, but it doesn't stop the journalists from continuing to pursue him at the collective. One of them is *BT*'s Torben Larsen, a previously good contact who often interviewed Lars and who now visits to find out what Lars is up to.

The sight of Larsen fills Lars with anger and anxiety. Here, he has isolated himself to get away from the media and the world that has frustrated him for so long, and they show up precisely when he needs them to stay away the most.

'I was standing in the kitchen and could see him talking to someone outside. At one point, I ran out barefoot, shouting and screaming at him to disappear,' Lars explains.

'I wasn't going to have him any closer. I had made an agreement with Hubbi, and when I make an agreement, I stick to it. He needed to go away so I could have peace and tranquillity.'

For family, friends, and football colleagues, it's shocking to read the media's reports about Lars's new life. Even in Råby, where Lars went from being the local hero to someone people don't quite know how to relate to. It's not that they blame Tage and Ingelise for anything. They haven't done anything wrong, and Tage's other son, Peter, leads an upstanding life. The local community also knows Lars as a good boy and a sympathetic person who willingly participated in events to the delight of the local community. So why this decision to isolate himself from the outside world?

At OB, Lars's team-mates are shaken by his decision. Some of them joke about planning to kidnap him, but as they acknowledge, he is a grown man making his own choices. And you can't force a man away from a place he has voluntarily chosen to be in.

Tage and Ingelise come to the same realisation, although they haven't given up hope of talking their youngest son out of his decision to live in the collective. They have nothing against Lars's spiritual quest, but they fear that the leaders of the collective will take advantage of Lars and his vulnerable position. Perhaps they will lure his money from him or make him do things he will later regret.

Above all, they love their son and fear losing him.

13

From Elstrup to Darando

WHILE THE world outside the collective wonders about Lars's change of life, his new daily routine slowly takes shape. But it's also quite radical.

As a symbol of the new beginning in their lives, it's common practice for new residents to change their names upon arriving at Sangha. The leaders, Hubbi Heiming and Knud Kløvedal, go by the names Premda and Shendo, and on their recommendation, Lars becomes Darando.

The name means 'the river flowing towards the sea' and is not chosen randomly. Lars yearns for freedom in the same way a river flows out into the open sea. He likes the name and the symbolism behind it.

Darando – a new name for a new start.

Strict structure

The days in Sangha are tightly structured, and Lars establishes a completely different daily routine than what he was used to.

Every Sunday, Hubbi outlines clear guidelines for the week's various practical tasks, where everything is organised collectively: from basic cleaning to gardening, maintenance, grocery shopping, cooking, and clearing up.

In Sangha, everyday practical tasks are seen as an essential part of spiritual development. Upon his arrival, Hubbi makes it clear to Lars that if one wants order within oneself, one must first and foremost establish order in the external environment.

'In this way, doing something physical becomes working on oneself. For example, by organising one's belongings and keeping track of things,' Lars explains.

'When living together as a community, there are also plenty of daily responsibilities to take care of. Laundry needs to be done, cleaning needs to be carried out, and meals need to be prepared, just like in any other home. Here, we take turns doing these things.'

In the collective, everything belongs to the community, which means that residents' private cars can also be used by other residents, with payment for fuel.

'The cars were communal, and you could book them to use. It cost two kroner per kilometre, and that way, the car was fully utilised,' says Lars.

'And when we needed to go shopping, a car would be sent out. We would find the cheapest place to shop and fill the car with groceries. We did this twice a week, buying supplies for all 40 residents.'

But practical work is not the only way in which the residents of Sangha work on themselves.

Exhausting sessions, intense reactions

Throughout the week, various meditation and therapy sessions are offered, allowing participants to work on different aspects of themselves. For example, there are the Tuesday groups, where dynamic meditation is taught, and there are the Thursday groups, where residents can seek advice from Hubbi regarding their personal problems. Additionally, film evenings and lectures are organised.

One of the therapy forms practised is called 'flushing', where participants release pent-up inner emotions through breathing exercises, wild screams, and shouts. For Lars, it becomes a powerful experience. For so many years, he has buried his feelings deep inside. Suppressed them. For so many years, he has bowed his head, complied, and done all the things people expected of him. Countless times, with a stomach ache, he has cried himself to sleep after being scolded by Tage for disappointing him on the football field. Now, it all bursts forth from within him.

These exercises bring out anger and sorrow in Lars. It's a cathartic but also very painful process. He screams out his anger, directed at his father, at unfair coaches, team-mates, friends, and others who have demanded so much from him over the years.

'If from childhood, one hasn't been heard by their parents or shown a path, it can fill them with aggression and introversion,' he says.

'In therapy, it's about getting these things out so that one can have some breathing room and feel oneself. There is a kind of truth in this type of therapy.'

These often exhausting sessions of 'shouting and screaming' for 30 to 45 minutes are usually followed by relaxing activities such as drawing or listening to calm music.

The therapeutic processing of all these repressed emotions begins to affect Lars's relationships with the people who have been around him over the years. He doesn't have much contact with his family, but when it does happen, the contact carries new and difficult emotions, and he struggles to handle this new side of himself.

The long-hidden anger is primarily directed at his own father and mother. Anger over not being heard, seen, or accepted. At least that's how he perceives it, and his reactions are intense.

Confrontation with parents

Tage and Ingelise Elstrup are shaken by the change in their son.

'He often called and yelled "I hate you!" over the phone. And it was really tough,' Tage recalls.

For Lars, it's a personal development that he now dares to confront his mother and father, to tell them what he feels and express his anger over what he perceives as a betrayal. But for the parents who love their son and believe they have given him the best, the anger is difficult to handle. Especially coming from a son they previously knew as gentle and caring.

However, it's not only Tage who gets to experience this new and angry side of Lars. One day, Ingelise goes down to visit Lars. She misses him, is worried, and just wants to see him. If she can't get him out of the collective, she can at least visit him there. But the meeting is brief and unsettling.

Upon her arrival at Sangha, she parks the car in the courtyard and steps out of it. She sees Lars and other residents walking towards her. She greets him with a 'Hi Lars,' but he doesn't respond to her greeting. Instead, he coldly stares into her eyes and says, 'You never meant anything to me!'

Together with the other residents, he continues past her as if she doesn't exist. Shocked and hurt, Ingelise sits back in the car, drives home slowly, and sits down sobbing at the kitchen table. Tage comes home and puts his arm around his wife. They both know the pain, and it brings them closer together.

Shortly afterwards, the phone rings again at Tage and Ingelise's home. Lars is on the line, and the message is short.

'You will not inherit me,' he informs Tage, who responds, 'But we don't want to inherit you, because that would mean you're dead.'

Tage is shaken as he hangs up the receiver. Why is their son now talking about inheritance? Have they ever asked him for his money? Besides the satellite dish Lars bought for Tage to watch English football, they have never received anything big or expensive from him. Not that they ever demanded it. They earned their own money, and although Lars has earned millions of kroner as a footballer, that's not what interests them. He is, first and foremost, their son, and that's all that matters. So, why this talk about inheritance? Neither Tage nor Ingelise feel they can recognise Lars. But it's not anger they feel. It's a deep sorrow and powerlessness. Every day Lars spends in the collective, they feel like they're losing a small part of the person they once knew and loved.

14

The Converted

LARS FEELS the changes happening within himself and in his entire life during the autumn of 1993 and into 1994 – in Sangha, in his relationship with Hubbi Heiming, and in the disconnection from his parents.

With Hubbi, he has found a woman he can talk to about things other than what he could talk to the girls he previously knew about. Hubbi is also a determined lady who, the year after Lars's arrival, breaks away from Michael Barnett and Wild Goose Company. Instead, she decides to continue the collective as an independent entity, changing its name to Solens Hjerte (Heart of the Sun).

'When Hubbi and Knud broke away from Michael Barnett, most other Sangha residents did the same. Including me,' says Lars.

'I no longer went to France for courses as I did in my first year in Sangha. I no longer read his books or followed his teachings in any other way.'

Breaking away from Barnett and his organisation is a significant step. Much of the inspiration for Sangha's therapy and teachings was derived from there, and Hubbi and Knud Kløvedal encouraged residents to seek knowledge from him.

However, there is no specific explanation for the separation, and even today, Lars cannot say what the reasons were.

'I don't know why. Perhaps it was Hubbi's desire to stand on her own feet? Maybe she disagreed with him on how things were presented? Maybe she thought she could do it better?'

More questions, fewer answers. But what is certain is that the separation gives Hubbi even more power. Previously, she referred to Barnett as the ultimate authority. Now, she is even more in control, determining the direction of the collective on her own.

In practical terms, the separation means that the collective has to move from the property in Højby. Instead, they find a base in the old nursery in Holmstrup, 10km south-west of Odense. The sale is financed as a cooperative purchase, with some members buying shares in the property.

However, everyday life doesn't change significantly. Lars and the others still live under primitive conditions, although the mobile homes are replaced with rooms. The daily practical work is still abundant. It even takes on a new dimension as the old nursery provides greater opportunities for cultivating the land, and Hubbi demands that plants and trees be cared for. Although the area is already beautiful, it can be made even more so.

As a result, Lars and the other residents have their hands full with renovations and maintenance of the new buildings. After a short time, the red-brick buildings appear well-maintained and tidy, the lawns are mowed with the precision of a golf course, and everywhere, flowers and old trees bear witness to immense care and attention. From morning to evening, hedges are trimmed, grass is cut, cleaning is done, all in an attempt to attain inner peace in Solens Hjerte.

TV2 moves in

On 25 October 1994, the TV2 programme *De Omvendte* (The Converted) airs. In a one-hour documentary, the Danish public get a glimpse into Lars's new life, portrayed by journalist Henrik Madsen, who knows Elstrup from his time as a journalist covering Brøndby IF. Madsen has lived in the centre for a week, observing the activities and daily lives of the members, including the most prominent member who motivated Madsen to make the documentary.

'The programme probably came about because of my move to Sangha, as I was a nationally known figure and moved into something mysterious, into a cult,' says Lars.

'Henrik Madsen showed interest in that story and asked if I would participate. I said yes, and then he had a conversation with Hubbi and Knud about the practical arrangements.'

The programme shocks and offends viewers at the same time. Most find it difficult to see the man they remember as the European Championship hero and football star dancing in what looks like ecstasy, calling himself Darando, and talking about a diverse range of spiritual matters.

This is the public's first real insight into Lars's new life. The tabloid press has sporadically tried to provide its readers with insight into his stay in Solens Hjerte, but it has been challenging. Lars has continued to be reluctant to give interviews. He just wants to be left alone and find himself in his new life.

Although the media's interest has been significant, several writers of letters to various newspapers in the weeks before and after the documentary wonder if Lars actually needs the attention of the press. One person writes, 'Regarding Lars Elstrup's new life, there are some of us who couldn't care less whether he is a member of the Beagle Boys, the Conservatives, or the Wild

Geese. But why does Lars Elstrup have a need to flaunt his new life? Is it because he can't do without the media's spotlight?'

The idea for the TV portrait does not originate from Lars or anyone in Solens Hjerte but from Henrik Madsen. The truth is that Lars still prefers to avoid the media's attention. However, when he does appear in the documentary, it's because he has nothing to hide. He is not ashamed and does not see himself as someone who needs to be 'rescued' from where he is. And he doesn't really care if people understand that when they watch the documentary. He just wants to show that he is doing well and doesn't need help.

Among the viewers this evening are Tage and Ingelise. It has been six months since they last saw their son. The last time was during a visit to the collective, which ended in anger and irreconcilability. Three months before the documentary, they spoke to Lars on the phone, but their contact remains sparse.

The parents miss him and are worried but still hold a faint hope of someday getting back the Lars they remember. It sends a chill down their spines when Lars says in the documentary, 'Here I will stay for the rest of my days.'

Tage sinks even further. It is precisely what he feared would happen when Lars moved into the cult.

Necessary brainwashing

In the documentary, Lars doesn't hide the fact that he has been 'brainwashed', but he also explains that it is a necessary process to be able to 'move forward'. When the broadcast ends, Tage and Ingelise sit silently but shaken, looking at each other.

Several journalists call to get their reaction. The parents don't really want to talk to anyone but end up speaking to a reporter from *BT*, with Tage saying, 'It was tough. A strong experience that needs to be processed. There are probably no parents who have it easy in such a situation. When they see their son in a completely different world. A world they don't know or understand. I feel that the documentary shows that there is a lack of love in Lars's life. We were searching for love but didn't find it. He said he was nervous and insecure during his time as a football player, but that's news to us. But there were many things that surprised us, many situations that we don't understand. Hubbi Heiming and Knud Kløvedal? No, we won't comment on them. It's Lars, and only him, who matters to us, and I'll end by repeating the wish to meet him. I can't believe it's over.'

In the following days, the phone rings incessantly for Ingelise and Tage. Some journalists want a comment, and there are also calls from people who want to help get Lars out of Solens Hjerte.

It's not always easy for Tage and Ingelise. Although many of the enquiries are well-intentioned, there are also some who become almost outraged if their advice is not well received.

But for the parents, it becomes increasingly burdensome as the phone rings many times every evening.

'All those idiots who kept calling,' says Tage with irritation in his voice, pausing for a moment. 'Some were compassionate and well-meaning, and just wanted to help, which was very nice of them. But it ended up being annoying to receive one piece of advice after another on how we should help Lars get out of the cult.'

Tage and Ingelise find that many other parents are or have been in a similar situation. People who, like them, have experienced the longing, frustration, and pain. And people who are willing to use desperate methods to save their children from a cult. Like the father who entered a religious commune and, armed with a hand grenade, dragged his daughter away from there.

Tage doesn't consider this option, but he readily admits that he is desperate to get his son away from Solens Hjerte.

Unpleasant calls

Tage and Ingelise also receive very unpleasant calls. One evening, the phone rings, and Tage only has time to hear a person hiss in his ear, 'You swine! How could you treat your boy like that?'

They receive several calls of that kind. The newspapers have published Tage's statements from Euro '92, where he talks about Lars and Peter being forced to run home after a bad performance on the field. Some media even believe that the direct cause of Lars's rejection of mainstream society in favour of life in Solens Hjerte is that he had a difficult and harsh upbringing. In the few interviews he gives during his stay in the collective, Lars also expresses that he had a challenging childhood. This causes certain people to react strongly.

'There were many who called and told me that I had forced the boys to play football and that I had beaten them and worse,' says Tage.

Solens Hjerte also takes precautions. One day, when Tage wants to have a talk with Knud Kløvedal in another attempt to get Lars out of the cult, Kløvedal has allied himself with a bodyguard. Just in case the rumours about Tage's violent side turn out to be true. Tage shakes his head. He might have the motivation to hit Kløvedal, but he would never actually do it.

However, there is one place where Tage and Ingelise can be free from all the rumours, threats, and unpleasant confrontations: among the villagers in Råby. Here, they never hear a single negative word. On the contrary; and local opinion counts far more than the national uproar.

Over the years, Tage and Ingelise have built up tremendous credibility and respect. Particularly through their daily work at the cooperative store, their social initiatives for the village children, and their enormous commitment to voluntary associations, especially IF Fjorden. The negative media portrayal does not change their reputation.

'People in Råby knew that Lars had a good and normal upbringing,' says Tage. 'And they knew that all those rumours about me "forcing them to play football and beating them" were false.'

However, even though Tage has a different perception of Lars's childhood than Lars himself and some media portray it, the negative articles still affect him.

'You still feel annoyed. Even though the people who matter and were close to me knew better,' admits Tage, adding, 'But there were a lot of people who called us, and it went on for a long time.'

Deeper wounds, greater distance

It will also be a long time before Tage and Ingelise see their son again. With so many bitter words and conflicts, the wounds become deeper and more difficult to heal. Tage and Ingelise still hope to get Lars out of Solens Hjerte, but they are starting to realise that the Lars they once knew may no longer exist.

Visits to Solens Hjerte can only happen on Hubbi and Knud's terms. And although the parents find the other residents of the collective to be kind and pleasant, they still feel that the two leaders are trying to create divisions between them and their son. They don't like them but are still at their mercy if they want to see Lars. It is solely up to them to decide who can visit the collective, and the answer is not always a mandatory 'yes' when a request is made.

For Lars, the family still exists. It's not that he doesn't want to visit them or has forgotten them. But he doesn't want to exert the energy it takes to visit them or even have them visit him. There are too many emotions involved, too much negative energy that needs to be processed, he feels.

It is also difficult for the rest of the family to handle Lars's new life.

Peter has difficulty recognising the accusations Lars makes against their parents. Peter doesn't feel that their childhood was as terrible as Lars has expressed. But like their parents, he also misses his brother when he's not busy with his work in a sports shop and his part-time job as a football coach.

Tage and Ingelise's relationship with Lars is summed up at the end of 1994 in an article in *BT* titled 'We Have Lost Our Son'. A dramatic headline, but that's how they feel in many ways.

And although they have experienced spending Christmas Eve without Lars before when he was occupied with football matches in England, this Christmas feels particularly sorrowful. The Christmas of 1994 is the second in a row that they spend without their youngest son, and unlike the previous year when they still had hope of seeing him again, they now feel that it might not happen.

As Tage expresses his and Ingelise's feelings at the end of 1994, when Lars has just become nationally known as the dancing Darando in Solens Hjerte, 'Lars should be allowed to live the life he wants, even though both Ingelise and I feel bad about his choices.'

And the new year brings no signs of regret from Lars's side. In 1995, he continues his life in Solens Hjerte and his relationship with Hubbi Heiming with little contact with the outside world.

15
A Black Hole

IT IS difficult to say exactly when it starts. Perhaps it begins in the spring when the sun's rays start peeking out more frequently, people come alive, and many become infatuated. Where the sun warms both body and heart, and endorphins gently massage the mind.

In Solens Hjerte, spring is also evident. Especially around the meticulously maintained flower beds and green budding fruit trees. The many hours of outdoor work give the residents ample opportunity to enjoy the light and air of spring and welcome the new season.

But for Lars, the spring of 1996 signals a change of a much darker nature. At this point, he has been living in the collective for two and a half years. He has found his place, knows his role and functions. He has had the opportunity to delve deep and take advantage of the spiritual exploration opportunities the place has offered. He has even formed a relationship with the leader, reaping the experiences and benefits it provides. In reality, he has all the prerequisites to finally find peace, joy, and harmony.

However, the anxiety and melancholy that plagued him throughout his football career are slowly starting to grip him again. It doesn't happen overnight. More like grey clouds creeping in and gradually overshadowing the sun. In Lars's case, the grey clouds in the sky quickly turn into pitch-black darkness without a hint of a ray of sunshine.

That's how it feels for Lars. Where he used to be able to smile and enjoy everyday life, everything suddenly becomes black. He feels depression pressing the zest for life out of him, without being able to resist. And it's not just a momentary melancholy.

'It was a new and stronger form of depression that I hadn't experienced before,' says Lars. 'Suddenly, I had no energy to take care of myself and just felt hopelessness and sadness, darker and more destructive thoughts, even suicidal thoughts.'

The recession of the mind

When does depression start? And how? Lars finds it difficult to say. But it gradually begins with more bad days than good, where Lars can handle less and less, physically, mentally, practically, and socially. He participates in fewer and fewer activities and eventually can't even muster the strength to leave his room or his bed. Getting up feels like running a marathon, and taking a shower becomes impossible. Personal hygiene is neglected. He has no appetite, no zest for life, no enthusiasm, and his once healthy and well-trained body slowly transforms into a withered shell.

'It probably happens gradually because it's not like one day you suddenly spend 24 hours in bed in your room,' Lars says as he begins a lengthy reflection on his depression.

'Or that one day, after participating equally in the daily work with the other residents, you decide, "I can't take it any more, I'll just lie in bed for 24 hours!" It's not like that.

'It's something that happens over a period of time where I withdraw further into myself and stop attending Tuesday groups, weekend groups, skip communal dinners, or stop walking our shared dog.'

Lars pauses for a moment and lets his banking-trained self continue with an analogy about the anatomy of depression.

'You can compare it to being a stockholder, where stock prices rise and fall. A company can experience growth and increasing earnings, causing the stock price to rise, or there can be a recession where the stock falls to a bottom level.

'But when can you say that the decline in stock starts, and why didn't you sell your stock at that time? And when does the decline stop, and when does the stock rise again? And why didn't you buy at that point? And when do you act and react?

'Afterward, you can always look at the graphs and say why didn't I just sell or buy there? But it depends on the understanding you have of the market and the company you invest in.

'And just like with the human mind: how much understanding did I have of the development at the time when my "stock" started to decline? Because I wasn't able to act or react to stop the decline, which I obviously would have liked to do.'

A third and equally significant question arises: why did he become so depressed as he did? Lars searches for a cause but doesn't find one.

'Things were going well for a while, and I don't have an explanation for why it went poorly,' he says, but then he adds, 'Maybe I wasn't heard, seen, or met in the right way, and then something happens to my psyche, and I retreat and shut myself in.'

Whether it was the lack of understanding from the other residents, the therapeutic processing of his childhood, or something entirely different, it's impossible to say. The inner demons have torn at Lars's mind before and since. Therefore, the explanation may not necessarily lie in Solens Hjerte.

But regardless of the reasons, it is a fact that no one in Solens Hjerte is able to reach Lars and help him out of the severe depression he is currently experiencing.

'I've locked myself in my room. I don't want to come out, don't want to talk to anyone, just have the food brought into my room, and that's it,' he says.

Naturally, the change is viewed with concern by the other residents, especially Hubbi, who has been closest to Lars, and her frustration is shared by others in the collective.

'People are worried. They want to help, and when you can see that the help you offer is not being received, it naturally becomes frustrating,' says Lars.

Hubbi seeks assistance

Time passes, and Lars continues to isolate himself from the outside world, including from the woman who is formally his girlfriend and spiritual guide. Frustration grows so strong within Hubbi that she seeks help from a rather unexpected source. Not only is she frustrated that Lars cannot or will not be helped, but she also feels that a more aggressive side of Lars is emerging, which she cannot handle.

One evening, the phone rings at Lars's parents' home. Ingelise answers the call, and this time it's not from strangers offering advice or hurling angry insults. On the other end of the line is the voice of the German-born leader of Solens Hjerte, seeking advice.

'He is dangerous! He choked me,' Hubbi's worried voice can be heard, without going into further details about how Lars is doing otherwise.

Ingelise doesn't know what to do. Her contact with Lars has been extremely limited for a long time, and she believes that his stay in the collective is doing more harm than good. Hubbi's current call doesn't exactly radically change her perspective. Ingelise has personally experienced how the stay has made Lars more aggressive and caused him to behave in ways that have shaken and surprised her.

So why is Hubbi calling her now? Ingelise still loves her son and doesn't want him to suffer. But what can she do? The Lars she knows has never been threatening or violent before. But the Lars she has come to know since he moved into the collective hasn't held back from yelling at her and Tage.

Not that she blames Lars for it. Lars is her son, and she loves him. But she blames the collective, and she blames Hubbi. It's Hubbi who has taken her son away from her. It's Hubbi who has turned him against his parents and everything he used to know and hold dear.

It's also the people in Solens Hjerte who claim to have so many answers and believe they have the means to help people. So why on earth can't they handle this, Ingelise wonders? Her voice sounds somewhat resigned as she says to Hubbi, 'Then you should report him!' With indignation in her voice, Hubbi replies, 'We don't report our friends.'

For a brief moment, there is silence on the phone. Ingelise finds it somewhat absurd that it now sounds as if she is the one who thinks her son should be reported. But she has no idea what else to say. The conversation ends, and Ingelise doesn't hear further from Hubbi or anyone else in the collective. Ingelise only knows that Lars is not doing well, and she is naturally worried. But she has been worried for so long now and feels that it can't get much worse.

But it can.

Suicide attempt

In the collective, Lars continues to isolate himself in his room, unable to comprehend the days. Slowly, day and night, week and month blend into a dense fog. Time simply passes, and Lars hardly knows which season it is. He came to the collective to find peace from his inner demons, and now they are more malevolent and larger, on the verge of destroying him. The initial time in Sangha was so exciting, bright, and rewarding, characterised by growth and progress, but now he feels worse than ever. And he is reaching a necessary conclusion for himself. 'I wanted to die, not live. I had nothing to offer to other people, and so I might as well disappear,' he reveals about the self-destructive emotions which drive him towards ending it all. He wants to take his own life, but most days, he doesn't do anything about it, mostly because he doesn't have the energy to plan and execute it.

Then one day, it happens that he has enough energy to get out of bed and even leave his room.

He walks unnoticed to a house on the premises known as 'The House of Spirits', which consists of some garages with a series of thick ceiling beams. Here, he can prepare undisturbed and bid his farewell to this world. He takes a rope with him and ties it securely to one of the beams and gets ready to hang himself.

There is no goodbye letter. It's just Lars, alone, broken, thin, tired and mentally done after months and months of non-stop pounding depression. He has nothing more to give in this life, nothing more to say. He just wants peace. He knows his suicide will gain a lot of attention, and some people will probably get sad. But he doesn't care about that now. He doesn't want to live any more. He's overwhelmed, feels no joy, and he has no joy to give to others. Or himself. Without joy life doesn't seem worth it. In death he must find peace of mind. He's ready to go. Just one move, and he'll be hanging, unable to breathe, unable to save himself from his own suicide. But he doesn't do it. Today, he can explain why he takes down the rope and goes back to his room, rather than finishing his life, right there in 'The House of Spirits'. However, it's not the last time he's close to taking his own life. 'I considered suicide during large parts of that period, and this episode wasn't the only attempt,' Lars reveals. 'I've also laid in a caravan there, with a knife, ready to cut my wrist.' Lars cannot explain why he stops the action then either, but he does, right before the knife reaches the wrist and finishes what no longer feels like a life. It's simply just basic survival.

His depression lasts for almost three years, during which he has no contact with his family and only minimal contact with other members of the collective. Naturally, his romantic relationship with Hubbi also ends. She is unable to reach Lars, and no one else can either. During this time, his life becomes a simple, basic survival day after day, month after month.

16

The Depression Disappears

IN THE summer of 1999, Lars starts to regain his joy. The depression vanishes just as inexplicably and suddenly as it had come, without any particular reason. Lars simply begins to regain control over his days, to dream, and make plans for the future again. He also considers whether those plans should involve the collective now known as Solens Hjerte.

During the autumn of 1999, he becomes more and more convinced that he needs to leave the life and home he has had for the past six years. He has had positive experiences in Solens Hjerte, but still hasn't found the peace he longs for. The nearly three years of depression have made him more critical of his surroundings.

Although he has experienced new and positive aspects of himself, learned things, and found words for many of the thoughts and feelings he couldn't express before, he has also realised that the strictly structured system in the collective is not so different from what he wanted to escape in the first place.

'Unfortunately, the stay didn't quite live up to what I wanted for my life,' admits Lars today.

'It was precisely the authoritarian framework and external expectations that I wanted to get away from, and Sangha and later Solens Hjerte are built around strict discipline, with the leader being the one in charge.'

'And I couldn't have found the peace I was seeking since I locked myself in my room for three years and refused to talk to anyone or participate in communal activities,' he says in a quiet acknowledgment that his depressive tendencies from his football career not only followed him but also intensified to a life-threatening degree.

But in the summer of 1999, when the depression finally releases its grip on him, he can once again manage his life and thoughts. He starts going out again, to the cinema and cafes, and interacts with people. These may seem like mundane things, but he lacked the energy for them in the previous three years.

Lars's deeper spiritual quest, however, is far from over. Soon, a new spontaneous inspiration will provide him with a new guiding path, all the way from Holmstrup to a holy ashram in India.

Inspiration in India

One autumn day in 1999, a small group of Solens Hjerte residents attend an event with the Indian guru Sri Swamiji in Copenhagen. Lars is not among them, but upon their return, they show him some photos of the guru and play his music on CD.

'The moment I see his picture and hear his music, I think, "I want to meet him, right away!" If it had been practical, I would have left that evening,' says Lars.

Instead, he spends the next few days obtaining a visa for India and checking transportation options to the guru's ashram in the southern state of Mysore.

A week later, he lands in Mysore. He finds the guru's sacred ashram, situated on a 34-hectare area behind 3m-high walls. Inside, there are temples, churches, prayer halls, therapy rooms, auditoriums, dining halls, kitchens, and cafes. Lars knocks on the gate, is let in, and proceeds to the registration office. He arrives unannounced but is still assigned a bed in a dormitory.

Even on his way to the office, he feels a healing sensation in his body and soul.

'A sense of calm comes over me, and I feel inner joy, relief, and even shed some tears. I feel a wellbeing because it's very different here, quiet and peaceful,' he reflects.

Lars has booked an open return ticket. He ends up staying in the ashram for 14 days, where in addition to the general wellbeing from the surrounding, he participates in the ashram's Navaratri festival, attended by a couple of hundred Europeans and around 5,000 Indians.

He listens to Sri Swamiji's lectures, gets to know some of the locals, and takes part in various meditation and therapy exercises, rituals, deity offerings, and singing lessons.

In just a few months, Lars has moved out of his room and into the vast world he never thought he would see again. The journey not only provides him with new spiritual stimulation but also gives him the courage for a significant life change.

Farewell to the collective

Upon returning from his ashram stay, Lars makes his final decision. He moves out of Solens Hjerte on New Year's Day.

He contacts an acquaintance from Odense Boldklub who rents out apartments, and shortly after, Lars gladly accepts a modest one-bedroom home in the town of Vissenbjerg. The conditions are not impressive, but after six years in a mobile home and later a room, followed by 14 days in an Indian dormitory, it is perfectly fine. Lars's definition of a sanctuary is not measured by square metres.

On 1 January 2000 he officially moves out of the collective, which happens without drama.

'I didn't discuss it much with Hubbi. You can come and go as you please in Solens Hjerte, there are no handcuffs,' he says about the situation today.

However, at that time in 2000, the tone was completely different. Shortly after moving out, Lars makes the following statement about Solens Hjerte and its leadership couple to *BT*, 'They just want to be in control. They can't let other people make decisions. That was the case when I chose to leave. They had a hard time accepting it.'

These words come in the context of a controversy that arises about six months after Lars left the collective as a resident. Although he no longer lives there, he still visits Solens Hjerte regularly to participate in activities, talk to the residents, or take walks with Devi, the five-year-old wire-haired dachshund he bought as a puppy. The dog is in the collective's care, so he must visit Solens Hjerte to spend time with her. However, one day he is told to stay away from the place.

'I don't understand them. I lived out there for many years and was part of their lives. When I moved away earlier this year, there were no problems visiting there. But now, it has completely changed.

'They asked me to stay away. I used to go there regularly to be with my dog and take walks. But I'm not allowed to do that any more,' he tells *BT*.

To this day, he still doesn't know what caused the sudden change in attitude, but he admits it was related to his interactions with the dog, and he struggled to control his temper in that regard. In a fit of anger, Lars throws a stone through the collective's large glass window and allegedly threatens Knud Kløvedal's life, although according to Lars, it was only his 'inflated ego' he wanted to harm.

At one point, the confrontation becomes so intense that his former housemates have to threaten him with the police before he decides to stay away from the collective.

Hello to the parents

On the other hand, Lars gradually reconnects with his parents. He has only seen them sporadically since arriving at Solens Hjerte and has had no contact with them during the three-year duration of his depression. But now he feels free and happy again. It gives him the energy to see his parents and create a space for himself where he can be with them in a positive way.

'When Lars moved to Vissenbjerg, we reached out to him, and then we started seeing each other a bit again. It was usually very calm and quiet, where we asked him if we could come and visit him. So we brought some food and other things, and we spent a couple of hours together,' says Ingelise.

Regarding the tentative reconciliation, Lars himself says in an interview from that time, 'I have contact with them again and understand and accept that we are very different. But after all, we are family.'

His plans for the future are uncertain, and he is slowly trying different things. He considers opening a countryside retreat similar to Solens Hjerte, where people can come and find peace. He also gives speeches here and there and considers accepting more. He writes stories about astrology and conversion and advertises therapeutic conversations on his now-defunct website.

He even manages to have a few client sessions because, as he says today, 'When you feel you have found something that was good for yourself, you want to offer your help and share it with others if they need it.'

Lars is on his way back, and in an interview with the newspaper *Aktuelt* at the time, he emphasises the significant shift in his mindset, where 'the desire to live outweighs the fear'.

And to such a degree that by 2000, he is inspired to make a comeback in both his football and love life.

An unusual comeback attempt

Three weeks after leaving Solens Hjerte, Lars starts to contemplate shocking plans. Now he wants to return to the football world he left behind with his infamous fax in the summer of 1993. There are a couple of months left until his 37th birthday, and he exudes a sudden belief that he can make a comeback in top-level football. He feels that his body and mind are in better shape than before, feeling stronger, more flexible, and mentally better equipped to handle the pressure that previously afflicted him and eventually broke him.

He has started to stand up to his father, whom he used to blindly obey. He now knows his own limits better, knows what he will tolerate and what he won't.

And he approaches the football world with a new-found openness, unlike his verbally restrained days as a powerful force in the national team.

'It's serious enough. I've thought about it, and I can still do it,' he says on 13 January 2000, when confronted with the absurdity of his plan by *BT*. And he continues confidently in the same interview, 'I have become much more flexible and agile in my body. I am in good mental shape, although, of course, I lack the football fitness to play two times 45 minutes, but that will come.'

Why?

In addition to sounding absurd to make a comeback at the age of almost 37 after a seven-year hiatus, it is also surprising that Lars now wants to return to the world that plagued his mind for so long. But he doesn't see it that way because his love for football itself remains intact.

'I have never blamed the game for affecting me so overwhelmingly negatively. It was my own fault for not being able to stand up to the constraints that made me depressed,' he asserts in the *BT* interview.

Most people in the football world shake their heads at the idea, but the main character himself has a much greater purpose behind his comeback attempt. It is not just about returning to the top level.

'My whole intention with making a comeback has been to show that it is possible to play top-level football without following the strict rules that characterise the football world. I firmly believe that with the help of meditation, stretching exercises, hot baths, and mental preparation, I can make myself even better than before,' Elstrup explains in an interview with *Euroman*.

'Even though I have grown older, I feel a greater lightness and a completely different harmony now than I did when I was at the top,' he continues, before dropping the bombshell, 'So my goal and dream are to play in the Danish Superliga without adhering to traditional training methods.'

Dreams versus madness

To the outside world, this may sound like sheer madness, but for Lars, it is important to dream again, something that was not possible during the three years he isolated himself in Solens Hjerte. Back then, it was simply about surviving each day. There was no hope, no dreams. While the world scoffs at dreams that seem far-fetched, for the main character, it is a victory to be able to dream again.

'I believe in it, but it will not in any way affect my life if it doesn't succeed. For me, it is important to be able to dream and set goals for my existence. If dreams don't come true, you just have to come up with new ones,' he says.

Part of the comeback project is therefore existential. But Lars also wants to test whether the experience and tools he has acquired over the past seven years can be used to enjoy football again without it being ruined by others' pressure and expectations.

'It's nice to kick a ball, and I still feel that way, and when it comes to being pressured, it will only be to the extent that I allow it. Unlike before, I now have some tools to say no, and my life is no longer dominated by other people's expectations,' he adds.

Thus, with clarity, Lars returns to the football world he had otherwise left behind, and it attracts just as much media attention as when he left.

While the news of his retirement was met with sympathy and respect, the decision to attempt a comeback evokes widespread astonishment. Moreover, the Danish Superliga clubs are not lining up to give the ageing striker a chance.

Back to OB

Although it may seem like an unrealistic project, OB's management agree to give Lars a chance. It is partly in gratitude for the efforts he previously made for the club. But there is also another, more selfish motive from OB's side. The club is currently lacking strikers, and perhaps even a somewhat diminished Lars can be the man to score some much-needed goals.

Team-mates are positive about Lars, but also highly sceptical. 'It's fine that he's trying to come back, and it's great that OB is giving him the chance. But my common sense tells me that after six years without physical training, it can't be done. Thirty-six years is a very high age for a top-level football player,' says the club's leading striker, Søren Andersen, when asked by *Ekstra Bladet* about the sensational comeback attempt.

But the bid almost fails before it even starts. It turns out that it is a different and far less humble Lars who shows up for the first training session. He is angry after an initial meeting with OB's management, who refused to pay him for his efforts. Lars doesn't see the trial at OB as an outstretched hand that he should gratefully accept. He has presented his financial demands to the OB management and believes that his name alone represents enormous PR value, which he believes should be compensated. He is therefore ice-cold when he tells *BT* on 19 January, 'I am very disappointed with OB's management's refusal to pay me for my completely justified demand for money to be back in the game. Look around! It's swarming with people from the print and electronic media. They have come to talk to me. The PR value for OB is enormous. The club receives a lot of attention, and sponsors' names appear on TV and in the sports pages.'

It's not that Lars lacks money. The rumours that he gave all his football earnings to the sect are pure fabrication. But just because he's a millionaire doesn't mean he has to work for free.

'When I wholeheartedly commit to an effort, I want to be compensated. They could, for example, start by paying me a daily salary, say 1,000 kroner,' says Lars before changing and preparing for his first media-covered comeback training session.

Support from a radio station

The remarkable story could have ended there, at the first training session. However, the radio station The Voice chooses to support

Lars's comeback attempt. It agrees to pay his salary while he trains with OB. Station manager Henrik Clausen explains the deal in *Ekstra Bladet* on 22 January, 'We want to support Elstrup's determination. And we believe that his ability to go against the current will interest the listeners. That's why we made the agreement.'

The deal involves Lars primarily doing morning radio for the station, which effectively means that his private sponsorship deal must not conflict with OB's sponsorship interests.

Thus, he continues training with OB for about a week before the final verdict is delivered by the club's management.

'I could not justify keeping Elstrup in the first-team squad, when some of our young players in the reserve team are more advanced at the moment,' says coach and sports director Torben Storm of his rejection of Lars. Although Lars has shown during training that he has not forgotten how to play football or score goals, Storm believes he still lacks a lot physically to be part of the team. 'It's a shame for Lars that he doesn't give it a little more time because he may indeed improve, but it takes time. It would be better for his body if he doesn't push too hard,' says Storm, leaving a small door slightly ajar.

However, Lars is not interested in that. He believes that OB's rejection is about something entirely different than his physical abilities. 'I am in good shape, and it keeps improving. I don't think it's so much my football skills that are the reason OB doesn't want to hire me. I don't think they can handle my personality and the way I present myself,' he states.

But OB's rejection does not cause Lars to give up hope. He declares, 'My goal is still to play in the Danish Superliga, and I will be ready when it starts on 12 March.'

He quickly has to abandon that dream.

Better luck with the blonde

Although Lars offers himself to clubs including FC Copenhagen, none is willing to take a chance on the veteran.

Instead, he reappears in far more humble circumstances when he joins the local Serie 2 club, Vissenbjerg, in late February 2000. Although he plays a couple of games, the club never becomes a stepping stone for a comeback career as a top player.

Instead, Lars is back in the role of a ladies' man. And this time, he doesn't need an intermediary or a gorilla suit to establish successful contact with the opposite sex.

Instead of playing in the Danish Superliga, he takes a couple of days for a relaxing trip to the Netherlands. Almost back home after the long drive, he decides to 'have a look around' in downtown Odense.

He enters the cafe and nightclub Franck A, where he spots an available chair next to a lone blonde. Polite, Lars asks if he can sit down, and the woman agrees. They strike up a conversation.

'And then we ended up together,' Lars says.

'I was really happy to be able to sit next to a beautiful blonde with a gorgeous body, a lovely smile, and big breasts. She was fresh and lovely, and she still is to this day.

'She looked damn good, and I probably did too in her eyes, hehehe,' Lars laughs with his disarming charmer smile.

'And when he's handsome, and she's beautiful, you want to spend more time together, and things naturally develop.'

In the case of Lars and the blonde, whose name is Gitte, they become serious and enter into a relationship that lasts from 2000 to 2004.

17

Blue Rope and Roller Skates

AFTER ABANDONING his plans for a comeback in top-level football, Lars begins to engage in other plans in the spring of 2000.

He feels good in his new home in Vissenbjerg. He feels that he has something to offer to the people around him. And he senses his intuition and spontaneity stirring within him. He is also outgoing during this period, and suddenly he has a compelling idea.

'One morning, I thought, "Now something damn well has to happen,"' says Lars Elstrup. 'And that's when the idea arose for me to try standing in the middle of the main pedestrian street in Odense. The place where the most people pass by. I wanted to show them something. Give them a message.'

The message is to be illustrated using a blue rope and a pair of roller skates. Lars plans to lay the rope in a circle on the ground, stand in the middle, and attempt to maintain balance on the roller skates he had just learned to manoeuvre in the previous five days. He hopes for a positive effect.

'The message is something I've heard and read about in books,' he says.

'It's about how as human beings, we each live within our own shell, and the blue rope is meant to symbolise that I am standing inside my own shell.'

The intention was for him to stand there on the pedestrian street without saying anything: to just be there and experience his own reactions and the reactions of the surrounding world. To feel himself and have an experience out of it.

And an experience it certainly does become. The performance quickly attracts attention, especially because Lars doesn't settle for just standing with the blue rope around him. He doesn't remain silent but addresses the passers-by with more or less appropriate – or, in some cases, inappropriate – shouts. He does it to provoke a reaction. To see how people respond to his words and his act.

And people certainly do respond.

Convicted of violence

While most people simply pass by in wonder or shaking their heads, three young boys around the age of 16 decide to test how far Lars is willing to go.

Shouts like 'shut up, have you seen that idiot?' are followed by 'fuck you, you retard', while Lars responds with verbal threats to 'get rid of the boys if they don't leave'. But when one of the boys finally shouts, 'Come out here and hit me if you dare,' Lars no longer believes that words are enough. Especially when the boy follows up with the retort, 'But a fool like you is probably afraid to come out of your rope!'

Lars is not afraid, as he proves when he steps out of his self-imposed confinement and delivers a resounding slap to the boy. This escalates the situation. Four security guards intervene and ask Lars to calm down. It's an invitation that he doesn't accept, as he is still agitated when a police car arrives shortly after. One of the officers gives him a gentle pat on the shoulder, but that's a move he should never have made. With adrenaline pumping through his body and angry that he is being seen as the guilty party, Lars reacts by striking the officer's arm.

Within seconds, Lars finds himself subdued by two officers. With his face pressed against the cold pavement of the street, he hisses at the officers, 'Damn, it hurts, man! Don't I have the right to a lawyer?' He does, but first, he has to take a trip to the police station.

The boys involved later tell several media outlets that it was Lars who had provoked and shouted at them. 'When we were a few metres away from him, he shouted nasty words and "I'll kill you" at me. When he told me I didn't dare come closer, I said I dared because I had the right to be on the pedestrian street. I told him he didn't dare to hit, but he did,' says one of the boys, who also mentions that they are all OB fans and have no intention of pressing charges against Lars.

However, the police do press charges, and the incident ends up costing Lars a conviction for violence. Three hours after his release, he is back on the pedestrian street, armed with his blue rope and his message.

Reflecting on the incident, Lars says, 'I remember there were some shouts, and I decided not to say anything. But then it clicked when the three boys walked by. Or, there had to be a response, or "they shouldn't be cheeky or smart". That's why I responded to them, especially one of them. He instigated it, and I played along.

'I had just learned to roller skate and was quite unsure. But when I rolled about five metres towards the kid and gave him a good slap, I was actually very confident on the skates.

'But I was in a place where I didn't think about the consequences, and it wasn't my original intention to respond or slap him.

'But then I ended up in court and received a conviction. And I found out that I could indeed roller-skate.'

Worried friends

Many view the incident as a sign that the former international player is truly losing it. Several friends and former team-mates express their concerns. One of them is Lars Høgh. Throughout the autumn, Lars has started calling his old team-mate again.

The phone conversations give Høgh a sense that Lars is heading towards a normal life. But he quickly realises that Lars has no desire for help.

'I've tried to help Lars, but I can't do anything more. I've understood the signals he's sending, and they indicate that he doesn't need help. And when a man doesn't want help, you can't help him. I've been closer to Lars than most others in the club, but I have to accept that he is unreachable now. I can't reach him any more. I truly wish that man could have a good and peaceful life again because he has become the complete opposite of what I remember him as. But I don't know what to do,' says the goalkeeping legend to *Ekstra Bladet* on 12 April 2000.

Already during Lars's comeback in the public eye and during training with OB in January, Høgh has advised his old friend to keep a low profile. It's advice that Lars certainly hasn't taken to heart.

'I gradually realised that Lars wasn't doing well, but by then, it was too late. The press already had a hold of him, which shook me a bit. Because it was obvious that he wasn't ready for the media circus,' says Høgh in the same interview.

Høgh is not the only one from OB who contacts Lars. The director of OB, Jørgen Bækkelund, also calls his former striker.

'After seeing the newspaper headlines, I contacted him to say that OB will always be there for him if he needs help. But I don't know if he needs help. Nobody knows if there's actually something wrong with Lars. When he visits the club, he seems happy and content. You have to dig deeper behind the facade to determine if someone is ill, and none of us down here can do that,' Bækkelund rationally states in the same edition of *Ekstra Bladet*.

Contrary to what Høgh and most other former team-mates and friends believe, Lars is actually doing well. At least according to himself. And he doesn't understand why people feel the need to 'help' him.

'I don't understand why people think they need to take care of me,' he says to *Fyens Stiftstidende* on 14 April, and adds, 'I was happy when Jørgen Bækkelund called, but I had to tell him that I'm fine and don't need help.'

He also doesn't have much regard for Høgh's statements suggesting that he might be sick. 'I don't want to waste energy on that,' says Lars in the same interview. He also asserts, 'It's as if people don't hear it when I say that I'm fine as I am and don't need help.'

Another person who wants to help is Hubbi Heiming. She also reads about the pedestrian street incident in the newspaper and decides to contact Ingelise Elstrup, who receives a specific suggestion from her son's former girlfriend and counsellor.

'She called and we talked back and forth, and finally, she said, "We should have him involuntarily committed,"' Ingelise recalls today.

Ingelise doesn't know how to respond. She has, to some extent, re-established contact with Lars. But unlike Hubbi, she is much more aware that she has no influence over Lars's choices and the life he leads. Ingelise has long given up on reaching Lars.

There was a time when she considered treatment and maybe even involuntary commitment as options for her son. But she has now put that behind her in an attempt to move on with her own life. She cannot devote all her energy and strength to helping an adult son who doesn't want help. That's a decision she and Tage have made.

It's a step taken to protect themselves as well. The help they can provide is having a meal ready when Lars stops by or being there when he is open to contact.

Lars is not committed to a mental institution. However, he immediately calls his mother when he hears about the conversation between her and Hubbi.

'So Lars called shortly after I talked to Hubbi. I had to hold the phone away from my ear because he shouted about "why I said he should be involuntarily committed",' Ingelise recalls.

'But I had never said that. Hubbi had said it. I just confirmed that if they thought it was a good idea, then it was probably fine.

'But it's just an example of how Hubbi sowed discord between us and turned everything we said against us.'

Lars's version of the story is slightly different.

'After my little event on the pedestrian street in Odense, I heard that my former girlfriend from Solens Hjerte had called my mother and recommended having me involuntarily committed. My mother thought it was a good idea,' he says.

'I strongly reacted to her and clearly told her what I thought of her actions. It resulted in the best and most intimate conversation I have ever had with my mother.'

Lars certainly doesn't feel any need for hospitalisation or treatment. After his long depression with isolation, anxiety, and suicide attempts, he feels, for the first time in a long while, free and full of life.

'I want to live. It's a persistent feeling inside me. I want to live more and more, and no one can take that desire away from me,' he states in the interview with *Fyens Stiftstidende* on 14 April.

His will to live and renewed confidence also mean that Lars is not particularly critical of what he chooses to say yes to. In November 2000, an unexpected opportunity arises. The talk show *Krudt i Kassen* on the TV channel Bio+ is in urgent need when it receives a last-minute cancellation from a scheduled stand-up comedian. In each programme, there is a visit from a comedian who gets four minutes of free rein, after which viewers can vote for their favourite performer. The winner receives a trip to London.

For unknown reasons, the people behind the programme contact Lars. Not surprisingly, the originally shy and introverted Lars has never performed comedy before. But in connection with the broadcast, he states, 'There's no reason to hesitate to live one's life. It's beyond comprehension. I only know two jokes, and we'll see what happens. Life is boring if you have too many plans.'

Thus, armed with two jokes and a lot of determination, Lars makes his debut as a stand-up comedian on television. The success may be modest, but it's not that important to Lars. He sees his participation as a challenge, and it's a challenge he has accepted.

And he'll manage to arrange the trip to London on his own.

Meeting Lord Nelson, having a good time with Gitte

The following year, Lars once again finds himself in the media spotlight. During a trip to London, he creates another so-called 'happening'. However, the English audience is not receptive to his alternative way of conveying his messages. This time, the blue rope and roller skates are replaced with a long floral dress, a Stetson hat, and a Danish flag. The message Lars wants to convey is spread this time on busy Trafalgar Square, right next to the famous statue of the naval hero Lord Nelson.

It's not unlikely that the real Lord Nelson would have turned a blind eye when Lars decides to discard both the dress and hat, and then proceeds to stand on his hands next to the statue, wearing only the not particularly covering Danish flag, which boldly proclaims 'ELSTRUP MEETS LORD NELSON'. But neither Lord Nelson nor the many people in the square are impressed. Shortly afterwards, Lars is escorted away by a large security guard.

Lars has come to London with a message and a mission, but just like in Odense, the performance has attracted more attention than the message itself. There is, of course, a greater purpose to appearing nearly naked in perhaps the most famous square in Europe's largest city.

'The purpose was to show that we are naked, that there is nothing to be afraid of. Whether one is physically or mentally naked, there is nothing to hide. One must stand by oneself,' Lars explains in an interview with *Tipsbladet* in November 2007.

After this episode, Lars becomes quieter. He mostly keeps to himself and leads a quiet life in and around Vissenbjerg. He enjoys the company of his girlfriend Gitte, who is a student in Odense and quite tolerant of Lars's small happenings.

'Yes, we were sort of half-boyfriend and girlfriend for about four years, where we were together and didn't see anyone else,' says Lars. 'She was very sweet and lovely, and when I told her about my happening with the blue rope, she simply said she definitely didn't want to witness it.'

Occasionally, they even engage in some casual football, just informal small-scale matches, now that he has realised his top-level career is over.

On the other hand, the troublesome depressions are making relentless comebacks. They have no age limit, they don't care about club colours, and they disregard physical fitness and positive periods.

18

New Downfall, New Beginning, New Depression, New Start

IN THE summer of 2007, Lars leaves the island of Funen, which has been his primary residence for the past 19 years. The last seven years were spent in a small apartment in Vissenbjerg, where he has lived since leaving Solens Hjerte. It's a drastic decision he makes after experiencing a new major downfall, which begins in the quiet spring of 2004.

Lars can't exactly pinpoint when the demons invade his mind. He rarely can. When the downturn begins, the start and end of the days merge together, and weeks and months blend into one engulfing darkness of the mind.

However, it has become almost obligatory that after a few good years, around three pitch-black years follow, where Lars is weighed down deeply under the oppressive yoke of depression.

In 2004, he doesn't escape either. Depression creeps back into his life and destroys his regained joy. He completely stops being social, no longer has the energy to travel the 15km (10 miles) to Odense, and cuts off contact with his parents once again. Living as a recluse, he hides behind drawn curtains. He orders most necessities online and only ventures outside the apartment when absolutely necessary. The apartment becomes cluttered, and Lars neglects both it and himself. The dishevelled apartment is a sad but symbolic representation of his chaotic mind.

Mentally, it's like a repetition of the three years of isolation in the room at the collective. But this time, there's no one bringing him food. No one knocking on his door. He is more isolated than ever before, and the few attempts by family and friends quickly fade away.

His relationship with Gitte in Odense ends during the early stages of his new depression. However, she tries to maintain some, albeit limited, contact with Lars.

'I withdrew more and more into myself. And those who reached out could sense that I didn't feel like talking. Eventually, they gave up because most of the time there was no response,' says Lars.

When he resurfaces after more than three years, he tells *Tipsbladet*, 'For three years, I didn't leave Vissenbjerg. I didn't visit anyone, and no one visited me. I only had brief conversations on the phone with my now ex-girlfriend Gitte and my mother. I played a lot of online poker and even won money, but it was an escape from reality.'

Back on track

One spring day in 2007, Lars can see clearly again. The grey clouds have left his mind, and he regains new energy, considering changes in his life.

He had experienced a similar feeling in 1999 when, after three dark years, he decided to move out of Solens Hjerte. Once again, he feels restlessness and the desire for a life transformation.

'I had once again gotten out of bed. I started tidying up my apartment and getting rid of things I no longer needed,' he explains.

To 'tidy up', he organises an auction at West End on Vesterbro in Odense. Fifty football fans show up and bid on various items of his memorabilia, including the 1992 European Championship gold medal, the silver medal from the Danish championship, and the cup title with OB in 1993. These are items that now hold no significance for Lars.

However, the purpose of the auction is not an urgent need for money. Instead, he has decided to donate the entire proceeds to the children's department at Odense University Hospital.

'I don't know how they do it at Bruun Rasmussen auction house, but let's give it a shot,' begins Lars, who acts as the auctioneer. Ultimately, the auction raises 17,000 kroner (jusst under £2,000) for the children's department, with the European Championship gold medal fetching 7,000 kroner.

It's a noble gesture, and at the same time, Lars has cleared out the old and the past. He is now ready to move forward in his life.

Originally, he doesn't plan to leave Funen. However, with his new-found zest for life, the need for social contact starts to arise again. Yet, he quickly realises that his social needs cannot be fulfilled in Vissenbjerg.

'I left my apartment door open and told people they could just come in. I also told the other residents in the building that they could let me know if they wanted a visit,' he recounts about this time, when barefoot Lars can be seen walking around his apartment, cooking, and inviting people inside.

His years in the collective still influence Lars, who now considers it natural to open his home to others. However, this thought isn't shared by the others in the building, and no one steps through his open door. Lars also longs for invitations to visit the other residents but is left disappointed when he discovers that people aren't as interested in social contact as he is.

Lars is no longer just the quiet and likeable football star and former European champion. His well-known stay at Solens Hjerte and his small, media-covered happenings have given him an unmistakable stamp as the village eccentric.

A trip to Copenhagen

Instead, Lars visits Copenhagen.

'I took the bus to Copenhagen with the purpose of maybe meeting someone. Just sitting down, having a cup of coffee, and talking to that person,' he explains.

Lars gets off the bus at the terminal just behind Copenhagen Central Station. He walks through the city centre and ends up in Nyhavn, where he encounters someone with time and a willingness to talk. It's the harbour master, Ib Hemmingsen.

While Lars and the harbour master enjoy coffee and conversation, Lars gazes out over the harbour and the many ships. Suddenly, he is struck by another spontaneous idea.

'After talking for about ten minutes, I noticed that there was a wooden ship for sale right next to where we were sitting,' he reveals.

'I went over to have a look at the ship, and by seven o'clock in the evening, I had bought it.'

Lars is now the proud owner of a boat in Nyhavn. The next day, he returns to Vissenbjerg only to pack up and arrange his move. He donates his furniture, television, and other larger belongings to Kirkens Korshær (a Danish charity that helps the poor, the homeless, and the other vulnerable groups) in Odense, keeping only a few possessions that fit on the boat.

Two days after his spontaneous trip to Copenhagen, Lars settles into his new home on the boat. In less than two days, he has moved from the small, quiet town of Vissenbjerg to the bustling

Nyhavn, one of the most popular and lively neighbourhoods in the capital. He thoroughly enjoys the sudden change. There's a vibrant atmosphere along the waterfront, and Lars relishes the contact with the many people there. It's summer, and he feels a warm inner joy that matches the summer sun.

'There was that feeling of freedom, which is central to me. And Nyhavn was just a really good environment to be in,' he says.

During this period, Lars gives an optimistic interview to *Tipsbladet*, expressing his happiness with his new life. 'I have no more anxiety,' he reveals, adding, 'Today's stress in society stems from anxiety because things actually move too fast, with no time for conversation, presence, and intimacy.'

However, summer turns to autumn and autumn to winter. Lars realises that a boat is not the ideal place to spend a Danish winter. It gets cold on the boat, and the buzzing harbour life gradually fades with the arrival of autumn. Consequently, he decides to only live on the boat during the summer. In November, he settles into a small attic room in a house in Holte, where he rents a space from an elderly lady. Before that, he plans another autumn trip to an inspiring ashram retreat and attends a course held by guru Sri Swamiji in Switzerland. Lars indulges his body and mind once again, seeking new positive experiences, learning new exercises and practices. The main purpose is to train the mind, feel wellbeing in the present moment, and thereby achieve a better everyday life. But consciously or unconsciously, Lars also desires to prevent new downturns in his life. Downturns that come suddenly and, at their worst, are life-threatening.

'I have no desire to fall into that black hole again,' Lars says firmly.

'Some time before I was about to travel to the ashram in September 2007, my ex-girlfriend Gitte visited me. We were sitting out on my boat in Nyhavn, and at one point, she said, "Don't fall into that black hole again, Lars!"

'And fresh and confident as I was, I said, "No, of course I won't!" But half a year later, I found myself back in that black hole.'

Rotting away in Holte?

In early 2008, Lars is once again struck by a severe depression. Despite declaring just a few months earlier that he no longer fears anxiety, it sneaks back in. It whispers like a cobra, saying, 'Who do you think you are? Do you believe you can escape from me?'

And then it strikes. Infecting his mind with a sudden darkness, complete surrender overcomes him. He finds himself in that same apathetic and meaningless existence. Spending his days lying on the sofa, unable to venture anywhere, suffering in body and mind. This time, it is in a secluded attic on Birkebakken in Holte, north of Copenhagen. It is a few kilometres away from the rundown collective in Ordrup, where he arrived on that tearful day of 1 January 1986.

'I had excruciating headaches and didn't dare go anywhere,' Lars reveals. 'For a period of eight months, I didn't dare venture into downtown Holte. Not even for basic grocery shopping. I ordered my supplies online. When I stepped outside the house, it was only to smoke a cigarette and quickly retreat back to my room. I had nothing to offer anyone. Life wasn't worth it. There was no one or nothing to be present for.'

After a meal, he easily spends eight hours on the sofa, just sleeping, sleeping, and sleeping. He can't bear the thought of getting up, going out, or even existing. Consequently, his contact with the outside world becomes minimal. 'During that time, I had such limited conversations with other people that the total minutes did not exceed an hour,' he recounts about the heavy period in the Holte attic.

Once again, this depression lasts for three long and exhausting years.

A different day

In August 2010, Lars's landlord, the old lady, passes away. From then until 1 February 2011, Lars lives alone in the house while the landlord's daughter, Mette, who is also a neighbour, spends the intervening time cleaning up and selling the house.

Lars is not much help. A few days before he has to move, his thoughts even revolve around suicide again. However, he had the presence of mind to receive the notice of termination of the lease and sublease a new apartment in the centre of Holte.

'I was knee-deep in shit and completely dark and disheartened. So it was a great effort just to drive my small load of belongings all the way to the new apartment. And I never thought I would overcome it,' says Lars.

'I remember thinking, "Well, it won't be here on Birkebakken that I'll die."' But then there is a sudden change in Lars's mindset. He has sorted out his move and feels that something has started to stir inside him. When he hands over his keys to Mette, they both say, 'It's like there's something different about today!'

During the relocation, he reconnects with his parents. The recent depression has resulted in sporadic contact between them, and in the past year, he hasn't spoken to his mother or father at all.

They are unaware of the dark state of mind their son is in. But one day they call him and become more informed. Lars may not be on top form, but at least he is receptive.

'We had no contact with him for a long time while he was living in Holte, and one day I called him,' says Ingelise.

'And it was completely coincidental because I had no idea things were so bad for him. He was about to move but wanted to come and visit us in Råby.

'He showed up looking terrible. He didn't have proper clothes and was so thin and worn out.'

But with the help of mother's homemade Jutlandic food and care, along with the good feeling of that different and improved day, Lars begins to feel a renewed sense of vitality. He is ready for a fresh start once again.

Reconciliation and regret

It's 2011 and Tage Elstrup waits at the bus stop at Randers Station, expecting Lars to arrive as scheduled on the bus at 8.15pm. But something must have gone wrong because the time has long gone beyond quarter past, and Lars is nowhere to be seen. Tage sighs. He starts to get worried but mostly irritated. Where is Lars? Tage looks out over the square once again. Still no sign of Lars. So, he starts the car and drives around the city to see if Lars might be somewhere else. But no luck. Tage can't find him anywhere. Finally, he decides to drive home with unfinished business.

Back home in Råby, the phone rings. It's Lars. He explains that something went wrong with the buses and that's why he arrived late for the appointment. He asks if they can pick him up at the bus station now. This time it's Ingelise who gets in the car and drives to Randers. Forty minutes later, Lars walks through the door of his parents' house and sets down his luggage. He notices his father, who looks annoyed at him, and with his familiar gruffness, remarks, 'When you say you'll be there by quarter past, then you damn well make sure you're there!'

Lars briefly looks at Tage, then at Ingelise, and says, 'I can't fucking stand being in this house!'

He grabs his luggage and walks out of the door he just entered. It's not the first time he has left the house shortly after arriving. Probably not the last either.

'I have learned to stand up to my family and to face the necessary confrontations, especially with my father, who has always been the head of the family,' says Lars, adding, 'And because of that, I think they have gained more respect for me.' When Lars is home for Christmas, and the roast pork is on the table, he can easily react impulsively and bluntly to a word or a sentence from Tage. He immediately gets up, puts on his coat, and goes over to the neighbour's house, asking if he can celebrate Christmas there.

He is no longer the shy and timid Lars, but a man with the courage to express his opinions. When he recently returned home to Råby for his parents' golden wedding anniversary, Lars taught his father how to properly pour wine and commented on the other guests. He particularly thought, 'They spoke too harshly to their children.'

Hates authority

Lars despises authority of any kind, whether it manifests in his father's anger over a delay or something as simple as waiting for a green light at a junction. He wonders why people respect authority so much, to the extent that they will, for example, remain at a red light even if there is no traffic. 'What are they so afraid of?' he asks.

He wonders about it, distances himself from it, and is not afraid to combat the passive belief in authority that 'stems from nothing but respect for authority itself'. Even in the midst of a breathing exercise in his inspiring abode at the ashram, authorities are not spared.

As a Facebook update from late 2011 emphasises, 'Yesterday, I attended my second session of Kriya Yoga Class here at the ashram in Mysore, South India. I arrived a bit late and forgot my white cloth, which one must wear when the session starts [wrapped around the head – author's note]. After half an hour, we went through breathing techniques, and the teacher went around asking each student if they understood it correctly. Finally, it was my turn. The teacher asked, and I looked him in the eyes and answered "yes" while nodding. The teacher asked again, and I had to repeat myself with a "yes" and a nod. Suddenly, the teacher noticed that I didn't have a white piece of cloth on me, and he said, "Please wear a white cloth in class. When you are in class, you must wear a white cloth." I said "yes", got up, and left the session.

'I don't want to waste any more time on idiots who want everything to be perfect when they themselves are fucked up in the head and ass.'

That's how Lars feels today. He reacts to 'authoritarian behaviour', whether expressed by an Indian yoga teacher or his father. Or like that one time when Lars ended up urinating in the harbour just as the harbour tour boat passed by, 'To bring some joy to the harbour.'

Instinctively and somewhat childishly, perhap, he does as he pleases, and it often gets him into trouble.

In October 2007, he moves his sailboat to Tuborg Harbour, then to Vedbæk Harbour, and from May 2011 to Lynetten on Amager. However, after a while, the harbour master had to inform him that he was no longer welcome there because several other sailors had complained about his behaviour. He had repeatedly violated the regulations and allegedly been threatening. Lars doesn't fully understand it, but he has also learned the art of behaving. He straightened things out with the harbour master and the most affected sailor. The issues were resolved, and Lars still has his sailboat in Lynetten. But only 'on borrowed time', as he puts it.

The element of reconciliation

But Lars's life is not one continuous conflict. Yes, his temperament and slightly different view of boundaries occasionally get him into trouble, but there is also something reconciling about him and the life he leads today.

He has long since reconciled with Hubbi Heiming and Knud Kløvedal. Together, they have resolved the conflicts that arose after he left the collective, and Lars is not the type to spend time and energy holding grudges.

'You can hold grudges against people, but then you end up dwelling too much on the past, and it becomes difficult to live in the present. Instead of looking back on the past, we should focus on where people are now,' he says.

That mindset also means that Lars regularly visits Solens Hjerte. He has been there six or seven times since coming out of his latest depression in February 2011.

'I visit them when it fits into my schedule. Last time was for lunch, and we spent a couple of hours just sitting and talking and listening. It's nice to come to a place where there is time, energy, and space to talk. Many other places have so many taboo areas and topics that aren't being addressed,' he adds.

As mentioned before, his relationship with his parents still leads to conflicts. But today, their relationship is so good that it can probably be considered the best in a long time.

'Today, I have a good relationship with both of them because I have found something within myself that allows me to be myself and, in turn, have a good relationship with other people,' says Lars. 'Something that enables me to better respond to the negative or positive energy I encounter from others. Thus, the interaction becomes a good forum that is developmental for both parties.

'Both with my mother and father and with other people, I try to be receptive and see what is needed in the relationship. With some people, it means having deep conversations, while with others, it means having a beer, laughing, and goofing around.

'Everyone needs different things, and people are at different stages in their lives.'

Paternal regret

Today, Lars doesn't discuss with his parents the authoritarian upbringing that he believes has done him more harm than good. That topic is in the past, and there is an unwritten rule between them not to bring up old things. It's about the relationship they can have now: Lars with a renewed perspective on them, himself, and his past. Tage and Ingelise silently acknowledge that it's better to have interaction with Lars in the way he is now than not being able to be together at all. The longing during the many years he was in Solens Hjerte was much greater than the pain that arises during their occasional conflicts when they meet. His parents have also long let go of the pain from that time.

'For the first three months, I cried every night, but eventually, you build up a defence to handle everyday life and move on,' says Tage, supported by his wife.

'We truly shed our tears, but eventually, we agreed that Lars shouldn't ruin our lives,' adds Ingelise.

'That's why we chose to focus on the good things and good memories and let the rest go.'

However, this doesn't prevent Tage from humbly reflecting when the topic of their sons' upbringing arises.

'Peter has told me that I didn't praise them enough back then, and others have mentioned it to me as well. But it was because I wanted them to be better at what they were doing. But it's probably true that I didn't praise them enough,' Tage admits, sighing deeply. And as his eyes turn red, he adds, 'I loved the kids, but I probably wasn't good enough at praising them.'

It took him many years to come to that realisation. But it's an important realisation that he reluctantly arrived at, perhaps because it was Peter, not Lars, who said it to him.

For many years, Tage repressed Lars's accusations, aware that his youngest son had gone astray in Solens Hjerte. They were the ones shaping his perspective on his childhood in a different and more critical light. They 'brainwashed' him, plain and simple.

Tage doesn't downplay the influence Solens Hjerte had on Lars and acknowledges that the place has certainly done more harm than good. But he also knows that he used Solens Hjerte as a kind of defence mechanism against his own shortcomings. However, over time, he has also realised that even though Lars has made choices that neither he nor Ingelise approve of, their son may have had a point regarding his upbringing.

When Peter also, in a confidential moment, tells his father that perhaps he should have praised his sons more, Tage's defence mechanism begins to crumble.

It's a painful realisation, and it contributes to creating a somewhat awkward atmosphere between Tage and Lars. It's impossible to correct the mistakes that happened so long ago. Impossible to go back in time and change it all.

Perhaps that is precisely what brings the Elstrup family to the present? What allows the parents and Lars to accept their common hardships as a necessary evil in order to continue seeing each other.

Leaving childhood behind

Tage's realisation of the lack of praise doesn't make a big difference to Lars today. He has long left his childhood behind, and he doesn't hold any grudges either.

'When you grow up, all parents give their children the love they have. They do what they think is best and pass on what they have learned themselves. That's how my parents did it,' says Lars.

'There are some things from my family that I didn't receive, but on the other hand, I received other things.

'In other families, it may have been the opposite: maybe they received love, affection, and freedom, but there may have been a lack of structure.'

When you see Lars relaxing with his parents in their garden over a serving of strawberries and cold buttermilk on a hot summer day, it's hard to understand that their relationship was characterised by distance and anger for many years. But time has done a lot, and both parties have now learned that compromises are necessary if they are to have any kind of relationship.

Tage and Ingelise also feel that their relationship today is 'the best it has been in a long time'.

'The last few times he has been here, we really feel like we've got the old Lars back. He smiles and seems happier,' Ingelise says.

'Yes, he has told jokes,' adds Tage, 'which I haven't heard him do in 15 years!'

When the conversation turns to the future, both Tage and Ingelise express hope that Lars will eventually find more peace.

'We hope that he will have a normal life with a regular job and maybe start a family, that he finds something to occupy himself with,' says Ingelise.

Something that Peter has already done. Lars also sees him occasionally, although less frequently.

'He lives in his own world. The world of football has always meant a lot to him, and he really enjoys being with people in that world. But if I go home for Christmas, we meet, play a game of table football, have a good time, and enjoy each other's company,' emphasises Lars, who has been on the path to recovery for over a year.

That's also something Tage has noticed.

'I'm glad that Lars seems to be doing better,' he says. 'And if he doesn't run into any obstacles, I believe he's on the right path.'

Dreams and demons

It's mid-April 2012, and Lars has just moved out of his apartment in Copenhagen's Sydhavnskvarter, one of the city's more modest neighbourhoods. Right now, he 'doesn't have a place to stay'. He has spent a couple of nights in his car, slept on a friend's sofa in Odense, and occasionally stayed in his poorly maintained sailboat at Lynetten.

'The boat has mould and leaks, so it depends on the weather how enjoyable it is to live on it,' Lars explains. 'When it's raining, it drips in seven or eight places, and all the mattresses get wet. But if the mattresses are dry, it's possible to sleep there. And now, hopefully, the weather is going to get better, so I have a fixed place to sleep. It's nice to have that.'

Lars adds with a relaxed demeanour, 'But I have found a place to stay tonight, and I don't think about where I'll sleep tomorrow. It doesn't concern me today.'

These words are spoken at Faxe Tribunen, his old home ground at Brøndby Stadium, just metres away from the clubhouse where he signed his million contract with Feyenoord over 25 years ago.

On the field, Brøndby IF and FC Midtjylland are playing a largely uneventful Superliga match that struggles to capture Lars's interest. Instead, he sits and exchanges text messages with a new female acquaintance. However, he casually and calmly notes in the opening of the match that the Brøndby forwards are not holding 'their attacking line'.

'That's why their attacks aren't dangerous,' Lars continues, and his short analysis proves to be highly verifiable. Throughout the game, the former champions don't produce a single shot on goal, and in the final quarter, FCM score two goals to defeat the home team.

By that time, Lars has long left the chilly arena. Just 15 minutes into the second half he has gone to the stadium pub to have a cup of coffee, and then he drives to his overnight accommodation for the evening.

Still passionate about football

Football still occupies his thoughts. The night before, he sat on a friend's sofa, enjoying the matches of both Real Madrid and Barcelona in the Spanish league. And he looks forward to following the upcoming UEFA European Championship, 20 years after he himself participated with enthusiasm, goalscoring instinct, joy, and fear.

'I'll sit and watch the matches with full focus. Enjoy the game and study how it is played today compared to back in 1992 and so on,' he says.

'But if there are kids who want me to play football at the same time, I choose that instead of watching football on TV.

'I love playing football and play whenever I get the chance. Whether it's on a real grass pitch, in the park, or on asphalt.

'I receive regular invitations, so I always keep my football boots in the trunk of my car, ready to go if the timing suits me.'

Recently, Lars played with some kids in a backyard in Nørrebro, invited through his Facebook page. Unfortunately, he had to cancel a seven-a-side match at Kløvermarken due to an interview appointment for this book. However, he had time to train some 15- and 16-year-old boys on the football fields in Brøndby, where the young Lars made his debut in full-time football.

On Christmas Day 2011, he even made a comeback in the most familiar surroundings when his old friend and fan, Christian Degn, organised an indoor game for the old friends from IF Fjorden. With a cancellation, Christian asked if Lars would join in, and he agreed. It was the first time in many years that Lars participated in an event in his old community. But at Christmas 2011, he was there again. And he thrived.

19

The Sanctuary of 2012

LARS IS in a good active period. He has also worked a couple of times at an after-school programme in Copenhagen. He has enjoyed working with children and has received positive feedback on his work, but he probably won't become a full-time educator. However, he is happy to act as a volunteer substitute.

He continues to offer therapy because he feels he has something to give. But he doesn't have a regular job, and he doesn't need one either. He has what he needs. His spending is still modest, and his football earnings have lasted.

However, he is also generous in offering a cup of coffee or a beer for a meeting or before a football match. And he gladly shares his resources when he feels like it. Like that spring day in 2011 when he decided to donate 25,000 kroner (£3,000) to the Christian-driven Café Retro in Copenhagen. This was in sympathy with the work the cafe supports in the third world and in gratitude for being allowed to take a three-hour nap at the cafe on a cold winter day after a night out. Lars can also be found at various pubs. Not because he drinks a lot of alcohol, he doesn't, but he enjoys the atmosphere and still loves a good game of pool.

He also visits homeless shelters because he feels comfortable among the homeless, society's so-called 'eccentric individuals'.

He listens to their stories, asks about them, and learns from them because, as Lars puts it, 'It's often in meeting people who seem to have the least to give that one experiences receiving the most.'

All of this is part of the process Lars experiences as a human being. A process rooted in the relentless desire he had to find a sanctuary since his professional football career seemed to enclose his inner, intuitive needs.

But has he found that today? Has he found that sanctuary and realised his dream?

'Yes, definitely! Back when I thought, "If only I could have this sabbatical year," I had those inner images of travelling the world with a backpack and lying on the beach with a drink in my hand.

'But I carry that backpack with me now, and I feel like I'm "lying on the beach" as I sit here doing this interview. And I know I can go if I want to experience the physical beach. But I don't feel like I'm lacking anything because I create my own life and obtain what I want. I have achieved financial independence, but if I were to lack something, I try to seek it out or find it.

'Everything is temporary, and spontaneity and intuition characterise the period I'm in now, which has lasted a little over a year. But I also think about whether I should plan something, set goals, become more organised, get my things in order, and set something in motion.

'And should I rent an apartment in Copenhagen, Odense, or somewhere entirely different? Maybe buy the local inn in Dalbyovre!'

Lars laughs liberatingly and self-deprecatingly. He just turned 49, floating freely and independently on his own terms. One wonders if he has completely abandoned the common life platform of a middle-aged man – a romantic relationship?

Lars hasn't ruled one out, but he doesn't miss being in one either.

'Not right now, as I sit here,' he says. 'Each person has their own path to follow, and no path is truer than another. And a romantic relationship can be a great place to grow and journey through life together.'

As mentioned earlier, Lars's last long-term relationship ended in 2004.

The lid on the black hole

In three separate instances spanning three years each, depression has obliterated any good intentions in Lars's mind: 1996–99, 2004–07, 2008–11. Almost a whole decade, if you combine them, and much more if you add the melancholic periods during and after his football career. That's a very long time in a life that hasn't reached half a century yet. And what's worse, the inner demons know no time limit or quota. They come and go as they please, and since 2003, Lars hasn't experienced a full calendar year without at least one stage of depression.

Currently, however, he is in the longest good streak in eight years – 15 months – and even has the energy to look back with a constructive perspective.

When asked how he currently views the previous periods of depression, Lars responds, 'They now place themselves as good experiences when I look back. Something I can use, something I have understanding for, something I remember where I can see more details, and something I can talk about calmly.'

But how can such dark periods be 'good memories', one may wonder?

'That's because today I'm in a mental state where I'm less obscured than before. I have become brighter, so when I look back now, I understand what has happened,' he says. 'And I've been working on that more or less consciously since 1 February 2011, when things began to turn around: on the first day, you take one step, the next day you take two steps, the following day four steps, then eight steps, and so on, where things somehow work exponentially.

'For me, it's about becoming aware of the things I do and say. Where I can constructively use everything from my past so that I can feel good again in my body, mind, and soul.'

Various meditation exercises are now a daily practice for Lars. They take place both at home when he has one and elsewhere: on the S-train, in a backyard behind his preferred spot, Sailor's Home in Nyhavn, or by the railing in the same harbour. All of these practices bring him wellbeing in everyday life and act as a defence against the latent depression that always seems to be lurking, ready to pounce when least expected.

'These exercises are to do something good and constructive for myself, to heal myself and make myself more flexible, both physically and mentally. That way, I get in shape, feel fresh and alert, gain insight, learn about life, and become more open. It's beneficial, and it's something I will continue,' he says, exemplifying with the so-called balancing exercise, which sometimes takes place on one of the mooring piles in Nyhavn.

'That exercise gives me more peace and balance, and I can feel that I'm standing more calmly and less insecure than the last time.'

Still alive

Despite the difficult periods, Lars has refrained from using medical antidepressants or seeking psychological help.

'Drawing from one's own experiences is more valuable than listening to friends' good advice. That's what I do. I take action and experience things to gain a better understanding of myself and the world around me,' he says.

'But that kind of understanding can be found in many different ways. Some find it through talk therapy or a conversation with a friend, through cycling or running because there are a thousand different ways to find one's inner peace.

'Ultimately, we humans are luminous beings who may have become obscured. And the mind is the mirror through which we can see how much light each individual has found.'

And unlike many other modern multi-tasking and media-stressed individuals, Lars takes the time for frequent Facebook updates and working on his mind.

However, he is someone who has had death and the dark sides of life closer to him than many others.

It has taught him that life is fragile, and the material things that many strive for have limited eternal value. When it comes to spiritual searching, he is still on a journey, and as a traveller, he is aware that there is a limit to how much baggage we can take on the journey. Or as he concludes, 'When we die, we can't take anything with us.'

With that philosophy, the free-spirited Lars has chosen to live life with little materialism but to live it fully, as best he can. But he is also aware that he can be overcome by the dark clouds of the mind and sink into an abyss so deep that he never knows if he will resurface. But right now, in 2012 he is doing well. He thrives and enjoys sharing his life, experiences, and thoughts.

And above all, he is still alive.

Epilogue

A decade on – Revival of Luton and Lars

THE SUN is shining, and the Danish summer is slowly approaching on this day in the early summer of 2022. Carsten Fog Hansen, one of the two authors of this book is sitting in his garden, enjoying a cup of coffee with Lars Elstrup, who has just dropped by for a visit. It doesn't happen very often, so the greater the joy of reunion.

Lars has popped in a couple of times since this book was first released in 2012. But when such visits do happen, they provide a good opportunity for conversations about big and small things, about football and life, and everything in between, and of course, about the book, which Lars himself was pleased with when it was first published, despite it portraying his sometimes controversial actions in an honest and thereby not always flattering way.

'It's simply such a good book you've written,' he says once again. Carsten thanks him, and uses the opportunity to politely ask a question that holds more than average social politeness, considering Lars's many ups and downs in his 60 years of life in light and darkness, 'How are you doing?' He honestly and openly shares, as he always does; he talks about how it's good to resurface again after another one of those dark periods that have become so familiar to him over the course of his life.

When the book was published in Denmark, it garnered significant media interest, and Lars willingly participated, sharing openly about himself and his struggles.

It was clear that this openness also encouraged others to speak candidly about their own challenges, performance anxiety, and the courage to pause and reflect. But then the darkness descended again, and Lars withdrew from the media, from attention and the spotlight.

Until he reappeared one day in August 2016, hitting the headlines again and in all naked action. During a visit to his old home ground in Randers, he simply decided to run naked on the field in the middle of the match between Randers and Silkeborg in the Danish Superliga. What exactly happened: ten minutes into the second half Elstrup entered the pitch from one of the main terraces, jumped over an advertising barrier, and in full monty he was heading to the halfway line. On his way making a gentle, Asian-minded gesture with his hand palms folded together over his head, like the *namaste* tribute in Nepalese tradition (from ancient Indian Sanskrit, 'I recognise the Divine within you'). Then arriving into the centre circle among puzzled players pausing the game, where he exercised some kind of yoga-style head stand with his feet up in the air. All that before a couple of stewards calmly escorted him out of the pitch. Out of visibility. With speechless players, staff and spectators left in a shockingly surprised state of a somewhat unreal experience just happening right in front of them. Not to mention all the non-speechless media there, capturing the whole scene, including of course the photographers.

For many outsiders, it was an undeniable sign that Lars had gone completely mad. But for the person himself, it represented the ultimate liberation, the ultimate defiance of external authorities and pressures. Difficult for the rest of us to understand, most likely, but it made sense in Lars's universe. And as he subsequently wrote on Messenger to one of the authors of this book, not without a good sense of humour, 'Now there seems to be plenty of material for a sequel of the book.'

As for his relationship with Randers, he apologised a few weeks later. In a statement (made in English on his Facebook page) he asked for 'forgiveness' for his act on the pitch, adding an offer for compensation to his former club: free half-time-entertainment featuring dance, good music and empathy conducted by Lars himself. 'I feel sorry for the inconvenience I may have caused,' he noted. However, Lars's offer never materialised, at his old home ground or elsewhere.

Afterwards, things quietened down around him, and the authors or the public haven't really heard much about him until now, where he's back, not in public, but sitting in one of the author's gardens, relaxing, enjoying the promising, mild summer breeze. The summer of 2022, with Lars turned 59 years old a few months before. He has tickets for tomorrow's FC Copenhagen home game in Idrætsparken, the national stadium, and plans to go. The fierce rivalry between Copenhagen and his former club Brøndby IF doesn't bother him. 'I've a good relationship with Lars Højer,' he says of the former Copenhagen and Denmark player, and current Copenhagen chief scout. 'He's always generous in offering me tickets.' Despite his rich experiences with the extreme sides of the mind, Lars has a bit of a hard time with antagonism in life, humans, culture – as well as in football, indeed.

He is calm, taking his time to talk to the author's children who eagerly greet the stranger who has come to visit. The author's football-loving son gets to kick the ball around with him, the former European champion, an honour he shares with Cristiano Ronaldo and Andrés Iniesta among others. And when both children serve an alternative meal they created in our kitchen, he kindly eats it so as not to disappoint them, smiling gratefully to each of them.

As they leave, both children exclaim, 'He was so nice, Dad.' The same observation is made by a Danish radio host later that year when Lars participates in a podcast focused on the summer of 1992. At the end of the edition, the host spontaneously exclaims, 'You're such a tremendously pleasant person to be around,' as if even he is surprised. 'Thank you,' Lars humbly responds. 'I hope I am, too.'

That's the other side of Lars that many don't see, not covered by the media, at least not very often. It's not as interesting as the scandals, the wild dramas, and the less flattering actions, but it's also who he is. Most of the time, actually.

The following year after our meeting in the garden, Lars travels back to Luton for the first time since he left, to the club and the town where he loved being, and where only personal battles made him leave.

Luton Town's resurgence is somewhat reminiscent of Lars's own. That club, too, was on the brink of destruction, as close as one can get. When this book was published in its first edition, Luton were outside the English league system. Now they are back in the Premier League, beaming with optimism, so it was fitting that Lars returned as part of his own revival, and was hailed by the enthusiastic crowd at Kenilworth Road during half-time of the match against Middlesbrough in April 2023.

Lars's return to Luton is met with warmth and enthusiasm from the locals. It's a mutual feeling. 'It's great to be back.

I don't like Luton; I love Luton,' he writes in a WhatsApp message to local journalist James Tuncliffe before they meet for an interview.

And as Tuncliffe later writes, in a piece for *The Lutonian*, while Lars certainly has his eccentric sides, meeting him is nothing like he imagined after hearing all the stories about him.

Lars is in a good place now. As he mentioned in the interview with Tuncliffe, 'For 30 years, I've been searching for this state of mind where I am free from anxiety and fear, and I've finally found it.'

What led him to this peace?

Lars attributes a significant part of his liberation from recent depression to the discovery of Sanatana Dharma (meaning 'eternal law'). Sanatana Dharma is the foundational spiritual philosophy that predates and influenced what we now recognise as Hinduism.

It's no coincidence, then, that the trip to Luton is just a segment of a larger pilgrimage with the primary destination being the Hindu Hanuman temple in Brentford. This temple is under the guidance of his spiritual mentor, His Holiness Parama Pujya Sri Ganapathy Sachchidananda Swamiji.

But will this freedom and peace last this time? Cynics might argue that Elstrup has been there before. That the peace is only a temporary ceasefire before the inner demons rise to fight again. Nevertheless, in the vast expanse of life's journey, hope endures, suggesting that a lasting place of serenity might truly be within his grasp this time around.

One thing is certain. Both 60-year-old Lars Elstrup and 138-year-old Luton Town strive for the same now: to rejoice in the resurgence and at being back at, or at least close to the top, to simply enjoy these times, as one appreciates the good moments even more when they have experienced the dark ones.

Facts and Statistics

Lars Dahl Elstrup

Born on 24 March 1963, in Råby

Playing career:

1981–85: Randers Freja – 136 matches, 59 goals

1986: Brøndby – 7 matches, 2 goals

1986–88: Feyenoord – 65 matches, 9 goals

1988–89: OB – 28 matches, 17 goals

1989–91: Luton Town – 60 matches, 19 goals

1991–93: OB – 44 matches, 24 goals

1988–93: Denmark national team – 34 matches, 13 goals

Bibliography

Interviews: Regi Blinker, Christian Degn, Ingelise Elstrup, Lars Elstrup, Tage Elstrup, Per Pedersen, Lasse Skov

Books:

Ankerdal, Steen & Werge, Carsten, *Peter Schmeichel – den bagerste* (Hovedland, 1991)

Barnak, Søren, *Brøndby IF – fordi de ville …* (Brønden, 2004)

Bruun, Morten, *11 år med dansk topfodbold* (Hovedland, 1999)

Heintze, Jan, *Tyve år på toppen* (Cicero, 2002)

Høgh, Lars, *Et fodboldliv* (Cicero, 2000)

Lundberg, Knud, *Europas bedste: Ricardos grimme ællinger* (Holkenfeldt, 1992)

Lybech, Arne (red.), *Fra Marken til Parken* (Lindtofte, 2005)

Povlsen, Flemming, *Europamester* (Allers Forlag, 1992)

Rasmussen, Jens 'Jam', *Formanden – Historien om Per Bjerregaard og Brøndby IF* (Peoples Press, 2009)

Carlsen's Football Yearbook editions from 1988 to 1993 (edited by Allan Margolinsky, published by Carlsen)

Newspapers/magazines:

A range of articles from local newspapers, as well as major Danish and international newspapers, including *Politiken*, *Tipsbladet*, *Euroman*, *Aktuelt*, *Morgenavisen Jyllandsposten*, *Fyens Stiftstidende*, *Ugeavisen Odense*, *Horsens Folkeblad*, *Information*, *Randers Amtsavis*, *Berlingske Tidende*, *BT*, *Ekstra Bladet*, *Algemeen Dagblad*, *Daily Mirror*, *The Lutoninan*, *Daily Mail*, and *The Guardian*.